Food & Thought

Food & Thought
home cookin' the healthy way

BY FRANK OAKES & FREEDOM TEAGUE
WITH AN INTRODUCTION BY ALFIE OAKES

COPYRIGHT 2012, 2015 Tiburon Press, Naples Florida

CONTENTS

introduction · **1**

Juices and Smoothies · **9**

Breakfast · **19**

Salads · **33**

Soups · **57**

Simple Sides · **73**

Vegetarian · **93**

Poultry · **113**

Seafood · **131**

index · **152**

INTRODUCTION

My earliest personal recollections all seem, in one way or another, connected to food - growing it, picking it, retailing it, watching Mom Mom Burris can and pickle it. By the ages of 6 and 7, my brother, Mitch, and I were waiting on customers, culling tomatoes and potatoes, bagging corn, and raking the bare soil that was the "floor" of my grandad's Pine Tree Market in Townsend, Delaware. Mom Mom would take us along to the King Street Market in the big city of Wilmington to help her sell fresh produce and eggs, homemade chow chow, and pickles to the city folk. And we will never forget the three hours at sunrise of frantically picking enough fresh corn to get our markets supplied through the day! This might be a good time to publicly come clean about the fact that my brother, Mitch, was indeed a faster and better corn picker than I was, and yes, even better than the legendary "Warwick Scotty."

My dad, "Banny" Oakes, who could aptly be described as perpetually animated and exuberant, broke from the farming and production side of the business to the marketing end, which fit his personality perfectly. To watch Dad operate at a roadside market was the greatest education my siblings and I could receive. In retrospect, it was a magical experience.

Food and Thought is the 20th retail store and farm I have owned or managed. Many lessons and memories of each and every one remain with me to this day. There were also two wholesale produce operations that supplied restaurants - ranging from little mom and pops to the largest in Southwest Florida. Over these six decades, I have seen the seeds change, the varieties of fruits and vegetables change, the way food is grown change, the way it is processed change, and the way it is prepared change.

Looking back to the 1950s, I remember the food my grandpa grew, the food my dad marketed, and the food my mom prepared for us. And I believe it is an urrefutable fact that the food was better, fresher, and more nutritious then.

Essentially, our cafe is wedding the best grown, most nutritious food in the world to time-tested, unadorned recipes, perpared in the healthiest manner we know. We are incredibly blessed to be able to grow and access the best food in the world and doubly blessed to have someone preparing it how my mom and grandmom would have loved and admired; but then, everyone loves and admires our kitchen magician, Freedom Teague.

Frank Oakes
July 1, 1946 - February 3, 2012

Freedom Teague
FOOD & THOUGHT COOK

As the oldest child in a family of 11, I began cooking at a very young age, creating my own recipes and experimenting in the kitchen. Each time I created a recipe, I jotted it down in a journal. At age 9, my family moved to a farm in Belize. We sold our Naples home and moved to a 20 acre farm where we grew everything we ate. Families would come and learn from us about how to farm and live off of the land.

At the time, our family ate only raw foods, but I began eating cooked food without my parents' knowledge. I learned to cook rice and beans over a fire from our neighbors. After several years, we moved to an Amish community in Central America. During that time, I discovered much about cooking rich, delicious foods and using what we had to create whole food meals. I learned to make butter, cheese and bread from scratch, beautiful pies, and other delicacies.

In 2002, I moved back from Belize and began working for Frank Oakes. In 2004, we started Food and Thought, which brings me so much satisfaction because customers enjoy the quality and variety of food we prepare.

As a cook in an organic café, I believe that high quality, organic food should speak for itself. As you read this cookbook and put together some of these meals, you will notice that we don't add hard-to-find ingredients or use complicated methods to put our meals together. Rather, the flavors of the food itself shine through.

Enjoy!

Alfie Oakes
FOOD & THOUGHT OWNER

There are many words I could use to describe my father, Frank Oakes -- he worked hard, he loved deeply, he ate heartily, he valued conservation and self-sustainability, he cared for his employees, and always sought the best for those around him. When I consider my father's life and legacy, one word comes to mind: My father was passionate! Passionate about his family, his conservative values and ideals, education, music, well-written books, and of course his incredible passion for organic farming and food.

My dad's passions intersected with an obvious need for health and wellness in our community -- to meet this need, in 2004 he created what was his life-long dream, Food and Thought, a militantly organic market and café with a peaceful, unique environment in which 100% organic food would be accessible to everyone. His incredible passion to provide organics to the Southwest Florida community allowed him to work tirelessly over the next 8 years to expand the footprint of the store to over six times its original size to deliver food, clothing, household items, and so much more to the employees and customers he loved so dearly. He designed Food and Thought as an oasis at which anyone could gather in community and grow in health and happiness.

Our Food and Thought family will continue on as Frank's legacy — to passionately provide the highest quality, 100% organic food in a market and cafe where the love of people and passion for sustainability and wellness continues to permeate through this amazing environment that my father created. Our courtyard provides a beautiful backdrop for conversation, restoration, and nourishment. Our home-style kitchen crafts delicious and healthy food made with the best ingredients available, keeping our dedicated customers coming back for more. We hope you will enjoy the recipes you find in this book as you celebrate Frank's life and the legacy he left for all of us.

Alfie Oakes

Why Organics?

When people choose to eat organically grown food, they are choosing to ingest more minerals and vitamins, and they are refusing to ingest loads of harmful chemicals, antibiotics, hormones, and substances devoid of any nutritional value whatsoever. Thus, their bodies are receiving the nutrition they need to boost their immune systems, fight off disease, and maintain health and wholeness throughout their entire lives.

Throughout this book, we have included bits of information which will help you make informed decisions regarding the food you put in your body. There are vast differences between organic dairy and its conventional counterpart. Similarly, organic meats, fish, sugars, and other commonly used products are completely dissimilar to conventionally grown and produced foods.

Food has the immense power to heal or destroy. Organic foods have the power to heal, promote wellness, and create an environment for you to thrive. And, much of our food is not any much more expensive than its conventionally grown counterpart. Organic growing methods free from chemicals, herbicides, and genetically modified organisms are completely sustainable. The organic growing methods are friendly to the surrounding environment, as well as our bodies, and - dare I say - our souls.

As a former chemical grower and one who scoffed at organic farmers and organic consumers and doubted all of their methods and motivations, I have been blessed to see things from all sides. There is no "gray area" and no doubt that to be optimally healthy, we must eat organically.

It is far too lengthy a process to explain everything properly here in our cookbook, so we encourage you to visit our website at *www.foodandthought.com* and click on *Why Organic?* where you will find a more complete explanation of organically grown foods.

Why Sprouted Flour?

Sprouted flour has been soaked and sprouted properly, rather than simply harvested and milled. This creates a live food that, when eaten, digests as a vegetable. Sprouted wheat flour is never dyed or bleached and contains no added chemicals.

We consider products baked with sprouted grains as health building foods. The non-sprouted flour that we are all used to is never health building, even if the flour is organic. Sprouted flour contains 70% less gluten than conventional wheat flour, and as a complex carbohydrate, it provides lasting energy for the body. Rather than encouraging bacteria growth, it nourishes the body and promotes healthy digestion. Organically grown wheat processed correctly (soaked and sprouted) is the best choice for cooking and baking in terms of nutritional content, sustainability, and promoting healthy digestion.

CHOOSING GROCERIES

Not every town in America has a Food and Thought organic marketplace! So, for those who are not able to live in beautiful Southwest Florida, what are some practical ways to select high quality, organic food from the neighborhood grocery store? Here is a quick and helpful guide to navigating the treacherous waters of choosing food.

Choosing Meats

Conventional meat or meat labeled "all natural" is typically:
- Fed genetically modified soy and corn products, inconsistent with the animals' needs and grown without a view for sustainability.
- Fed a steady diet of hormones and antibiotics, so that animals grow abnormally large and resist the formation of sores as a result of being penned in so closely with other animals.
- Inhumanely slaughtered.

Rather than selecting conventional meats, select meat that is USDA certified organic and grass fed. This insures a proper balance of omegas, as non-grass fed beef is almost devoid of omegas. If possible, choose meat from a local farmer who understands sustainability and what is known as "friendly farming."

Choosing Salt

Conventional table salt (sodium chloride) sold at typical grocery stores is derived from unnatural chemicals. It provides no minerals or vitamins to the body, and increases levels of bad cholesterol in the body. The best salt for the body to ingest is whole sea salt, which is packed to the brim with minerals and creates an alkaline environment in the digestive system. This alkaline environment prevents diseased cells from forming. Use this type of salt for all recipes in this cookbook. Dr. Brownstein's, <u>Salt Your Way To Health</u>, is a book we think every food maker should read.

Choosing Fish

Select wild, line caught fish from Alaska, Iceland, Greenland, or other cold environments. These cold climates provide a cleaner environment, free from many bacteria in which fish grow and develop. These cold climate fish, which are wild caught with line, are smaller, containing much lower levels of mercury, if any. Fish frozen at the catch site have less chance for bacterial contamination than "fresh fish" that may be several days old. Salmon, halibut and cod are our favorites for health and cleanliness. Yellowtail snapper is the only fresh fish we serve here at Food and Thought when one of our local fishermen can get it to us the same day it's caught. Yellowtail is about the "cleanest" fish in our gulf waters. There are many government websites that "grade" different species.

Choosing Milk and Cheese

If at all possible, select raw milk and cheese from grass fed, certified organic dairies. These products have not been heated to high temperatures and cooled rapidly multiple times (pasteurization). Thus, they retain all the helpful bacteria, omega-3s, and enzymes. Organic, pasteurized milks and cheeses are also beneficial to the body. The cows and goats that have produced organic milk are fed organic food, have not ingested antibiotics to prevent sores, and have not undergone hormone therapy. Over time, cows that have ingested these types of harmful products become resistant. Additionally, the substances are passed on to those who drink conventional milk and eat conventional cheese, making resistance to antibiotics a growing concern. Hormone levels in milk impact the body's own ability to regulate hormone levels, causing early puberty and early menopause in women, and lowered testosterone levels in men.

JUICES AND SMOOTHIES

Juices and smoothies provide a great filler and lots of nutrition. Our juice bar serves lots of different juices, smoothies, and coffees. The recipes we've included in here are the most popular.

Our most popular drink at the juice bar, The Doctor, tastes great and is packed with vitamins and minerals.

The Doctor
CELERY, CARROT, BEET, APPLE

3-4 celery stalk pieces

3 carrots

1 whole beet

1 whole apple

½ bunch of parsley

½ of a lemon

1 small piece of ginger

Wash all vegetables and fruits. Place the items in your juicer, one at a time, ending with the celery. Stir your juice, and enjoy directly after making.

Preparing fresh pressed juices from fresh fruits and vegetables has endless benefits. Drinking juices on a daily basis is a very efficient way to get vitamins and minerals directly to your blood stream. Additionally, juices contain many enzymes - drink within 15 minutes for maximum benefit.

 If you need a shot of vitality and infusion of minerals without sugar, the green machine is the way to go! Use any leafy greens you have on hand - lettuce, spinach, kale, or chard. Enjoy this juice as it is, or add some pineapple cores or ginger for added flavor.

The Green Machine
CELERY, SPINACH, KALE

Wash all vegetables. Place the items in your juicer, one at a time, ending with the celery. Stir your juice, and enjoy directly after making.

3-4 stalks celery
1 whole cucumber
1 whole lemon
4 spinach leaves
4 kale leaves
½ bunch of parsley

" Say you are well, or all is well with you, and God shall hear your words and make them true "

- Ella Wheeler Wilcox

The Berry Nice is our most popular fruit smoothie. Use any berries you have on hand. If desired, add a scoop of protein powder.

Berry Nice
BANANA, STRAWBERRY, RASPBERRY

10 ounces apple juice
1 whole banana, frozen
6-7 frozen strawberries
A handful of frozen blueberries
Several frozen raspberries

Freeze fruit in season to use throughout the year. Place all ingredients in your blender. Blend on high, then reduce speed to low for smoothest results. Add more fruit or juice as necessary.

When various fruits are in season, buy in bulk. Rinse thoroughly and let them dry. Then, freeze the fruit in freezer bags, making sure to seal tightly and get as much air out of the bags as possible. Use the fruit throughout the year for smoothies or other recipes.

 Named for one of our sweetest customers, the Gentle Joe has a satisfying flavor. Use pressed coconut or pineapple juice for best results. We use organic Lakewood Juices for all of our smoothies, as they have no additives.

The Gentle Joe
BANANA, STRAWBERRY, PEACH

Freeze fruit in season to use throughout the year. Place all ingredients in your blender. Blend on high, then reduce speed to low for smoothest results. Add more fruit or juice as necessary.

10 ounces coconut juice
1 whole banana, frozen
6-7 frozen small strawberries
5-6 frozen peach slices
(the equivalent of one whole peach)

BREAKFAST

At Food and Thought, we believe breakfast is the most important meal of the day. Start your day by putting life giving, organically grown foods in your body. Our recipes are filled with fresh ingredients, such as sprouted wheat flour, eggs from free-range chickens, and colorful vegetables. Pair your own delightful breakfast with organic brewed coffee or herbal tea.

This delicious, gluten-free dish is one of our most popular breakfast items. Each day, we use the fresh vegetables that look the best to us. We enjoy using food when it is in season and readily available. Thus, the type of quiche we serve varies throughout the year.

Breakfast Quiche

EGGS, CHEDDAR CHEESE, VEGETABLES

8 organic eggs

2 cups shredded cheddar cheese

½ cup cream

½ teaspoon salt

½ teaspoon pepper

Chopped vegetables of your choice (broccoli, asparagus, yellow squash, zucchini, or spinach)

Preheat your oven to 350 degrees. Beat the eggs together with the cream. Add 1 ½ cups of cheese, raw chopped vegetables, salt, and pepper. Stir to incorporate. Dust an 8 x 8 inch glass baking dish with olive oil and rice flour. Pour the egg mixture into the dusted dish. Sprinkle the remaining ½ cup of cheese on the top. Bake for 35 minutes.

Organic eggs are hatched by hens who have the opportunity to run around a farm, explore, and live a very satisfied, active lifestyle. These hens eat organically grown chicken feed (not soy or corn derivatives), and as a result, their eggs contain higher protein levels with less harmful bacteria and chemical content. The yolks are bright yellow, and the whites are clear. They lay eggs when they feel like laying eggs, not when a hormone additive in their food tells them to lay eggs.

 Sprouted grains are life giving, and eating sprouted grain pancakes for breakfast is a great way to start the day. Frank's favorite breakfast was two sprouted grain pancakes with butter and maple syrup, along with a ½ teaspoon of heavy cream stirred into a giant mug of coffee. Make this simple recipe at home for lasting energy!

Sprouted Pancakes
SPROUTED WHEAT FLOUR AND BUTTERMILK

Mix together all the wet ingredients (water, egg, buttermilk, plain yogurt, butter, vanilla extract). Add in the dry ingredients and slowly beat together to incorporate. Cook pancakes over medium to medium-high heat.

2½ cups sprouted wheat flour
1¼ cup of water
1 egg
¼ cup buttermilk
¼ cup plain yogurt
2 tablespoons butter, softened
1 teaspoon vanilla extract
½ teaspoon baking powder
½ teaspoon baking soda
Salt
Just a tad of maple syrup

Breakfast

 These tasty muffins are packed with minerals and protein, found in the chia powder. For those intolerant or sensitive to gluten, these muffins are a great alternative.

Katie's Gluten-Free Chocolate Chia Muffins

COFFEE, BUTTERMILK, CHIA POWDER

Preheat oven to 325 degrees. Whisk together butter, maple syrup, vanilla, and eggs until thoroughly blended. Add the rest of the ingredients, and stir until mixed together evenly. Place muffin tin liners in the muffin tins. Fill a bit more than halfway with the mixture. Top with chocolate chips if you desire. Bake for 25 minutes. Yield: 12 muffins.

2 sticks of unsalted butter, softened
1¼ cups of cocoa powder
1 tablespoon vanilla extract
4 eggs
2½ cups coffee, cooled
2½ cups of buttermilk
2½ cups of white or brown rice flour
2½ cups of chia powder
2 teaspoons baking soda
2 teaspoons salt
2 tablespoons baking powder
1 cup chocolate chips (optional)

Try making a batch of these eggs for your entire family. The vegetables and spices complement the eggs and create a whole meal. Pair the Spanish-style eggs with sprouted grain toast.

Spanish-Style Eggs

EGGS, TOMATO, CILANTRO

8-10 organic whipped eggs
1 tomato, diced
½ of an onion, diced
½ cup cilantro, chopped
½ teaspoon paprika
Salt & pepper, to taste
Olive oil

Sauté the vegetables in olive oil over medium heat. Add in the eggs and cook to desired firmness. Add in cilantro and other spices at the end, and stir to incorporate. Serve immediately with sprouted grain toast.

 A favorite for breakfast, these muffins are best warmed in the oven and slathered with organic butter.

Sprouted Banana Nut Muffins
SPROUTED WHEAT FLOUR & BUTTERMILK

Preheat the oven to 325 degrees. Cream together the eggs and butter using a mixer. Add in the milk, lemon juice, maple syrup, molasses, palm shortening, and yogurt. Mash the bananas with your hands, and then add them into the mixture. In another bowl, combine the sprouted flour, salt, cinnamon, and baking soda. Slowly add the dry ingredients into the wet ingredients, stirring vigorously to incorporate with a mixer. Place muffin tin liners in the muffin tins. Fill each a bit more than halfway with the mixture. Top with chocolate chips or walnuts. Bake for 25 minutes.
Yield: 24 muffins.

12 ripe bananas
3½ - 4 cups sprouted wheat flour
3 eggs
1½ cups maple syrup
1 stick butter, softened
¼ cup plain yogurt
¼ cup milk
2 tablespoons lemon juice
2 tablespoons palm shortening or palm oil
1 tablespoon molasses
2 teaspoons baking soda
1 teaspoon cinnamon
A pinch of salt

Variation - Make into 2 - 9" by 5" loaves. Bake at 325 degrees for 45 minutes.

" If we could give every individual the right amount of nourishment and exercise, not too little and not too much, we would have found the safest way to health "

- Hippocrates

Yummy, pleasantly sweet, and free from conventional granulated white sugar! These muffins are oh-so-satisfying with a little butter and a mug of coffee.

Sprouted Carrot Muffins

CARROTS, SPROUTED FLOUR, MAPLE SYRUP

Preheat the oven to 325 degrees. Cream together the eggs and butter using a mixer. Add in the palm oil, maple syrup, and vanilla extract. Add the carrots and pineapple. In a separate bowl, combine the flour, baking powder, baking soda, cinnamon, cloves, salt, allspice, and nutmeg. Slowly add the dry ingredients into the wet ingredients until well combined. Stir in the raisins and walnuts. Place muffin tin liners in the muffin tins. Fill each a bit more than halfway with the mixture. Bake for 25-30 minutes. Yield: 24 muffins

4 eggs
½ cup butter, softened
¼ cup palm oil
1 ½ cups maple syrup
3 ½ cups shredded carrots
1 can crushed pineapple
2 teaspoons vanilla extract
2 ½ cups sprouted flour
1 teaspoon baking powder
1 teaspoon baking soda
1 teaspoon cinnamon
1 teaspoon cloves
½ teaspoon salt
1 pinch allspice
1 pinch nutmeg
½ cup raisins
½ cup walnuts

Breakfast

SALADS

Our "Grab and Go" case at Food and Thought is always filled with fresh salads and sandwiches made daily with organic ingredients. It is essential to select only organically grown and raised vegetables, dairy products, and meats. Many of these recipes are very simple and can be put together ahead of time, refrigerated, and enjoyed for about a week.

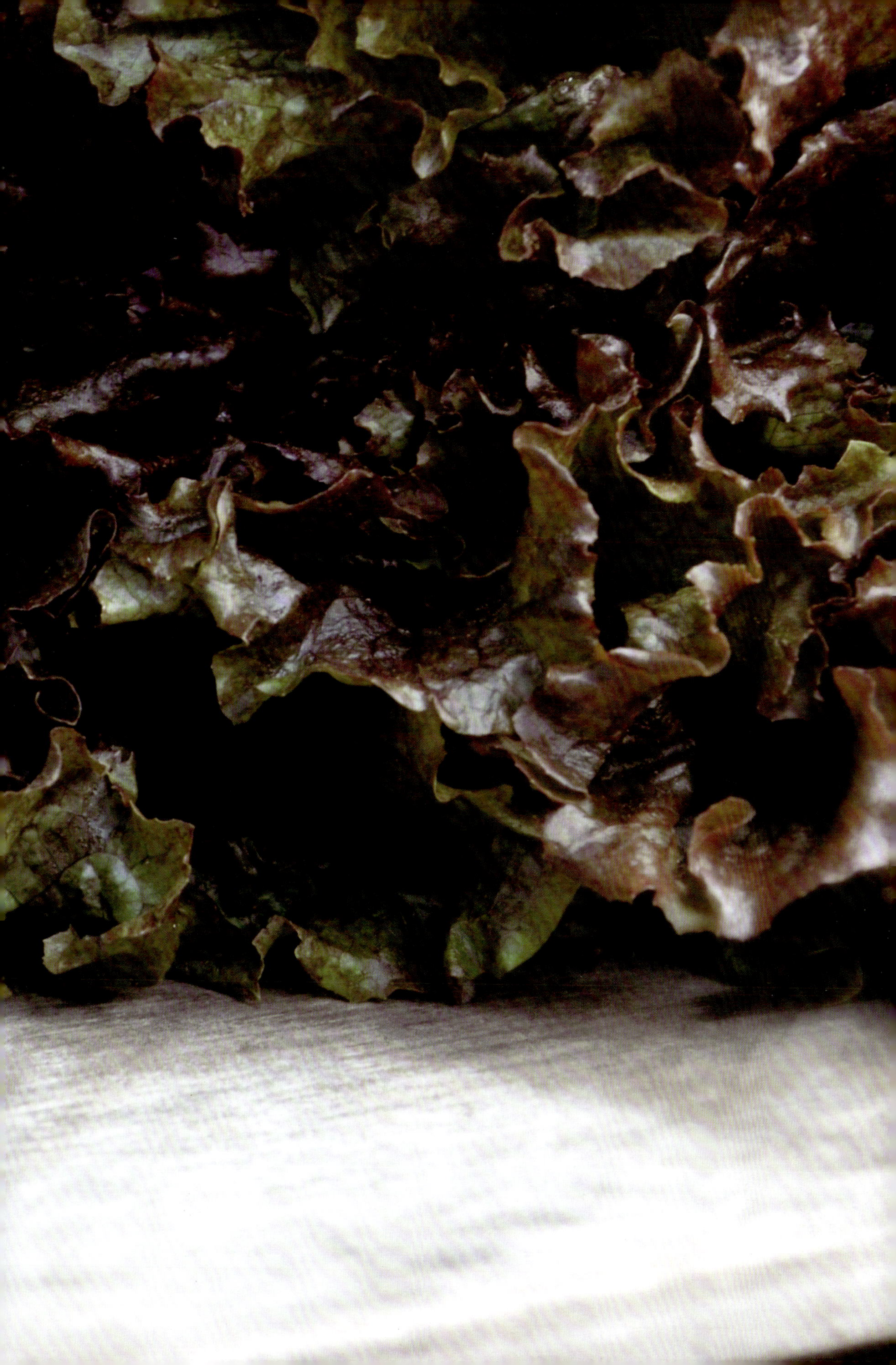

This salad is a popular, interesting alternative to traditional chicken salad. Put it on some toast with tomato and lettuce, or place it atop a green salad with lots of fresh veggies.

Grape Walnut Chicken Salad

CHICKEN, WALNUTS, GRAPES

4 cups boiled chicken breasts, chopped

1½ cups yogurt

1 cup green or red grapes, halved

½ cup walnuts, chopped

Salt and white pepper, to taste

Boil chicken breast over medium high heat for approximately 20-25 minutes, until done through. Let the chicken cool. Cut up the chicken breast, and mix in all other ingredients. Refrigerate in an air-tight container (preferably glass).

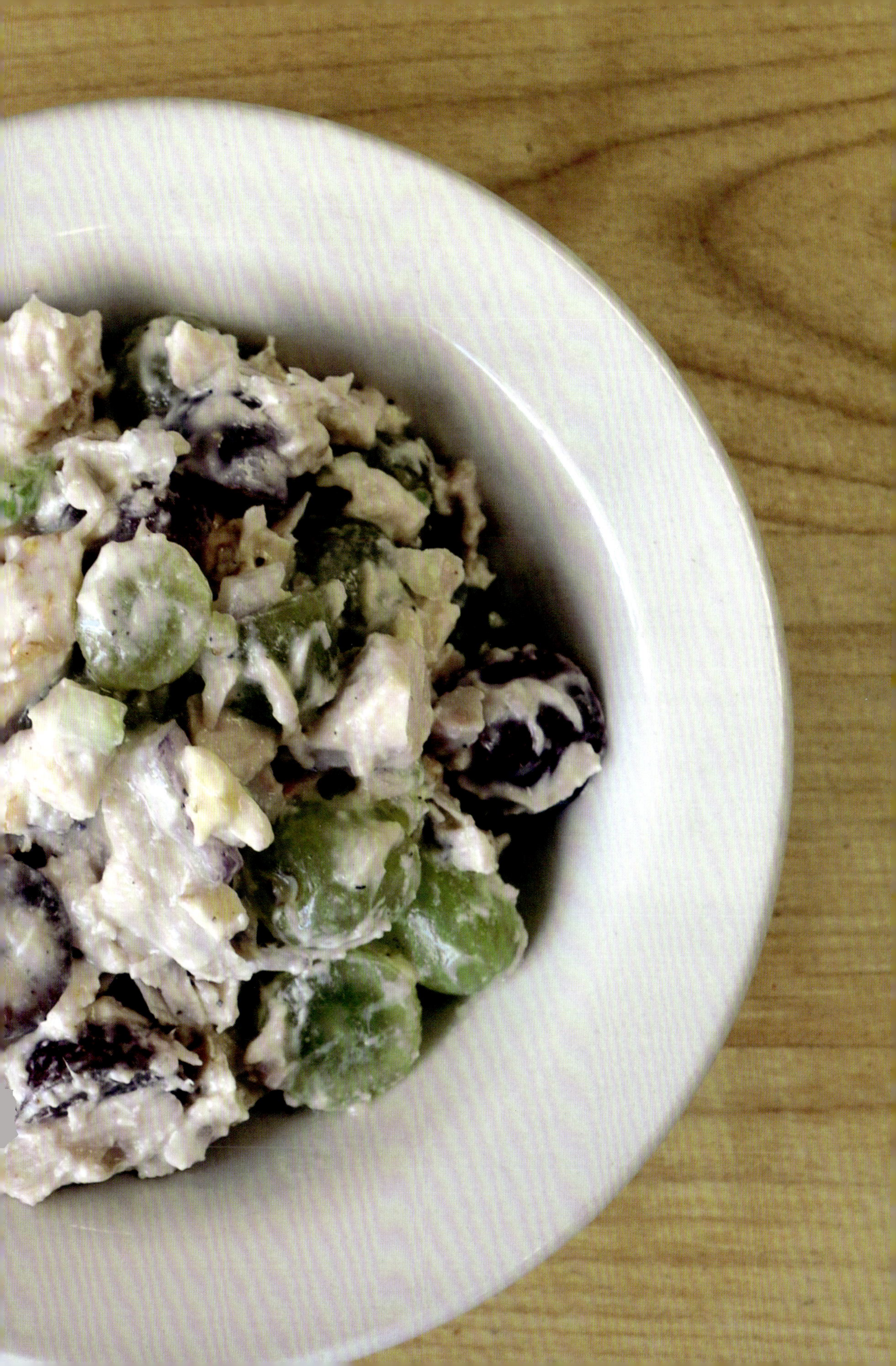

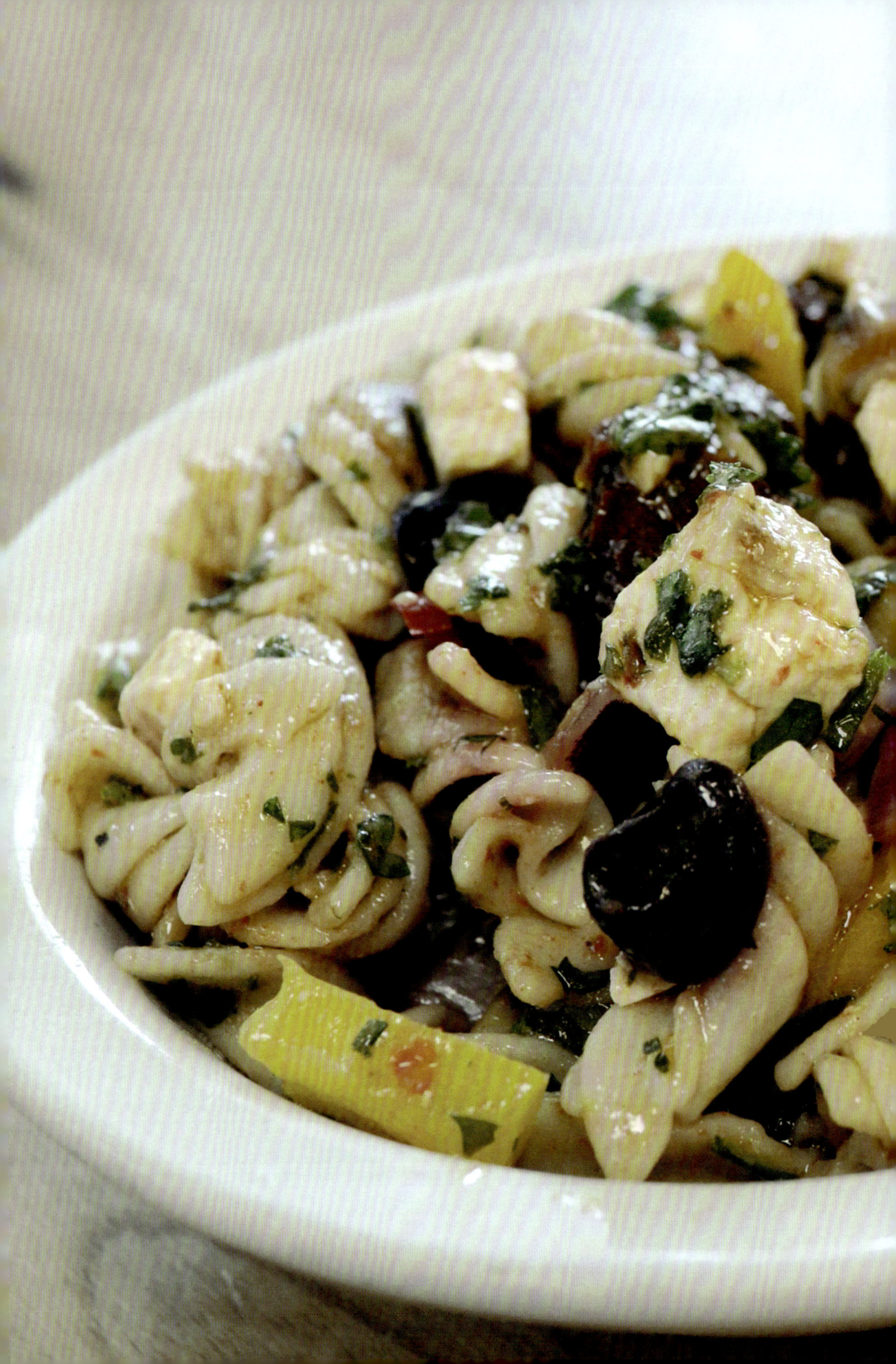

Pasta salad is a staple for summertime fun, but we make it the whole year through at Food and Thought. Group a batch of our pasta salad with grilled chicken breast and a chopped fruit salad for a fresh and flavorful evening meal.

Pasta Salad
BOW TIE PASTA, FETA CHEESE, BASIL

Cook the bow tie past per the directions on the packaging. Rinse the cooked pasta with cool water. Combine all of the ingredients in a bowl. Enjoy immediately, or refrigerate and store in an airtight container (preferably glass).

1 bag gluten-free pasta
4-6 ounces crumbled feta cheese
½ cup French dressing
½ cup peppers, chopped (yellow, red, or orange)
½ cup parsley, chopped
½ cup black olives, sliced
¼ cup red onion, chopped
¼ cup sun-dried tomatoes, chopped
1 teaspoon dried oregano
1 teaspoon dried basil
Olive oil and sea salt, to taste

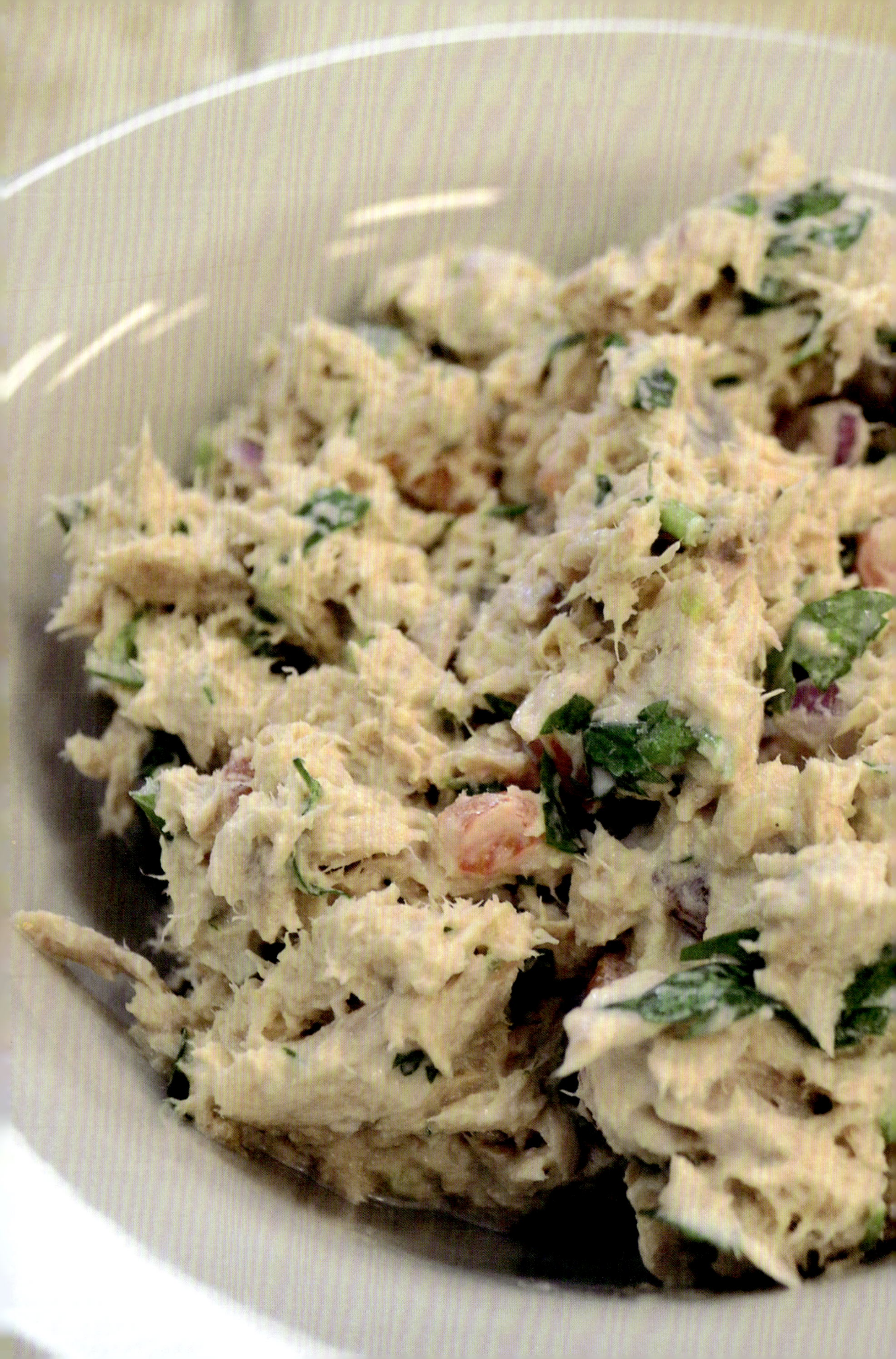

This spicy salad is a variation on traditional tuna salad. Adjust the seasonings to taste.

Mexican Tuna Salad
TUNA, TOMATOES, CILANTRO

Combine all ingredients in a large bowl. Enjoy immediately on a soft shell tortilla with sliced tomato and lettuce, or refrigerate and store in an airtight container (preferably glass).

2 cans tuna, drained
1 cup tomatoes, diced
¼ cup mayonnaise
¼ cup lemon juice
1 jalapeño, seeded and finely chopped
½ bunch cilantro, chopped
Salt and pepper, to taste

It is very difficult to find conventional canned tuna without added soy product, which usually contains genetically modified organisms (GMOs). Smaller tuna, such as Tongol tuna, contains less heavy metals and tastes the same.

Salads

This richly-colored salad is sweet and flavorful. It tastes best when allowed to sit in the refrigerator overnight.

Pickled Beet Salad
BEETS, CILANTRO, APPLE CIDER VINEGAR

4-5 medium beets

1 small red onion, sliced

½ bunch cilantro, chopped

½ cup apple cider vinegar

¼ cup olive oil

Salt and pepper, to taste

Boil beets until tender. Drain the beets and peel them. Slice the beets and cut them into quarters. Add in the remaining ingredients. Store the mixture in an airtight, glass container, and refrigerate overnight. The salad tastes best the day following preparation!

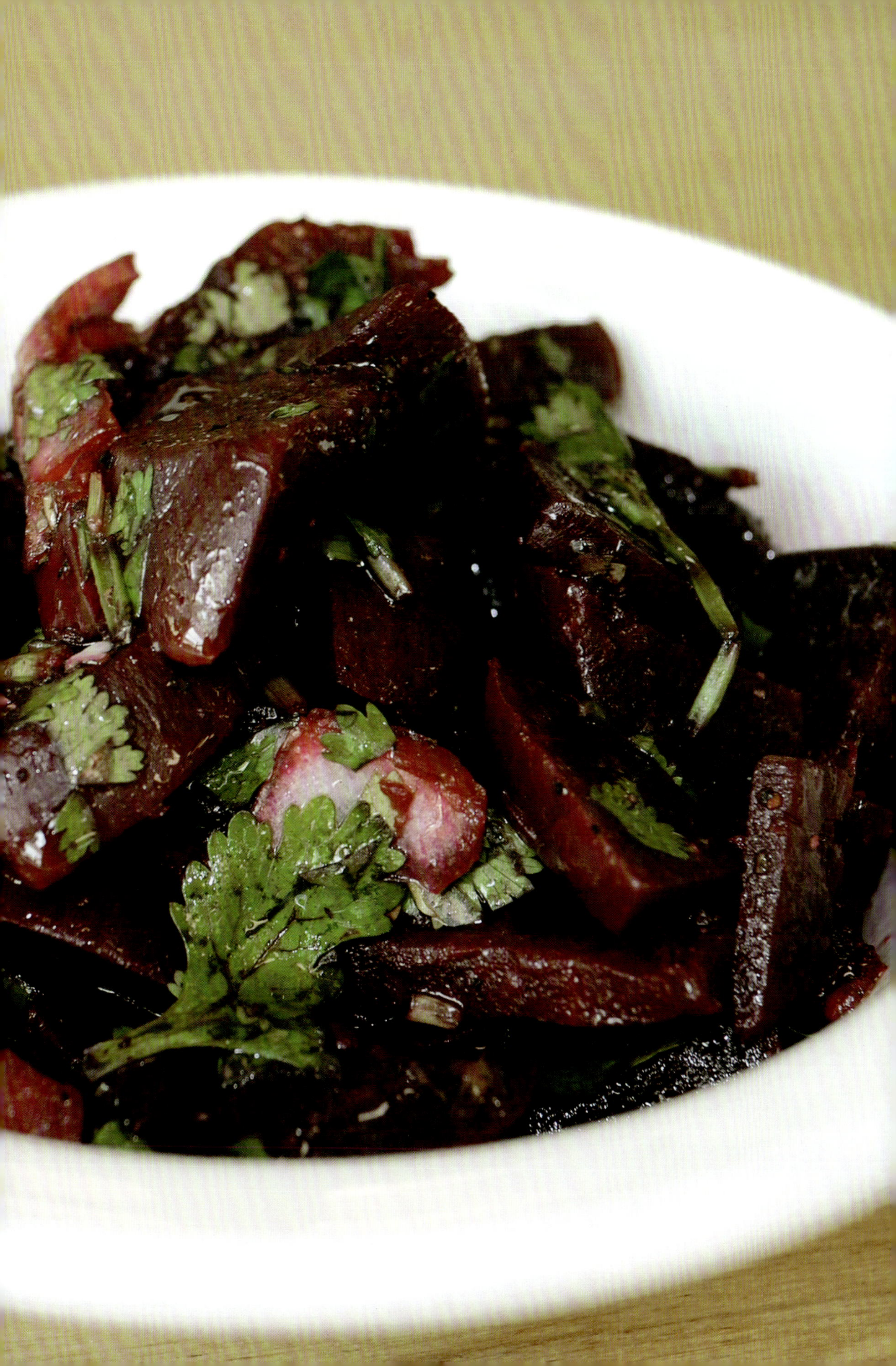

Canned beans are pressure cooked, which decreases the quality and nutritional content of the beans and can cause gas and bloating in the digestion process. Take the additional time to soak and boil beans; you will save money and increase the quality of your end product. As an added incentive, soaked and boiled beans have better flavor and are more economical to prepare.

Delicious and textured, our hummus is made from properly soaked, boiled garbanzo beans.

Homemade Hummus
GARBANZO BEANS, GARLIC, CUMIN

Soak the beans in a pot of water overnight. When you are ready to make the hummus, preheat the oven to 350 degrees. Rinse beans, and then fill the pot with water. Add some sea salt and a bay leaf. Bring to a boil, then reduce to a simmer and cook the beans for 45-60 minutes. During this process, roast the garlic by placing it in the preheated oven with olive oil for 10 minutes. Place the roasted garlic, cooked garbanzo beans, and all remaining ingredients in a food processor. Pulse the ingredients until the desired consistency has been achieved. Garnish with a touch of paprika and olive oil. Store the hummus in an airtight container in the refrigerator.

- 3-4 cups garbanzo beans
- 4 cloves roasted garlic
- ¼ cup olive oil, plus a few tablespoons more for roasting the garlic
- 2 tablespoons tahini
- ½ teaspoon cumin
- ½ teaspoon sea salt
- ¼ to ½ cup lemon juice, depending upon desired consistency
- A pinch of paprika

A yummy twist on traditional fruit salad, this would be a great addition to any meal - as a side or as a dessert!

Spanish Fruit Salad
APPLE, WALNUTS, RAISINS

1 red apple, cored and cut into chunks

1 green apple, cored and cut into chunks

1 cup plain yogurt

½ cup walnuts, chopped

¼ cup sweetened condensed milk

¼ cup raisins

½ cup red and green grapes, halved

Core the apples, and cut them into chunks. Chop the walnuts. Cut the grapes in half. Combine grapes, walnuts, apples, and raisins in a bowl. In a separate bowl, mix together the yogurt and sweetened condensed milk. Combine all ingredients together. Refrigerate in an airtight container.

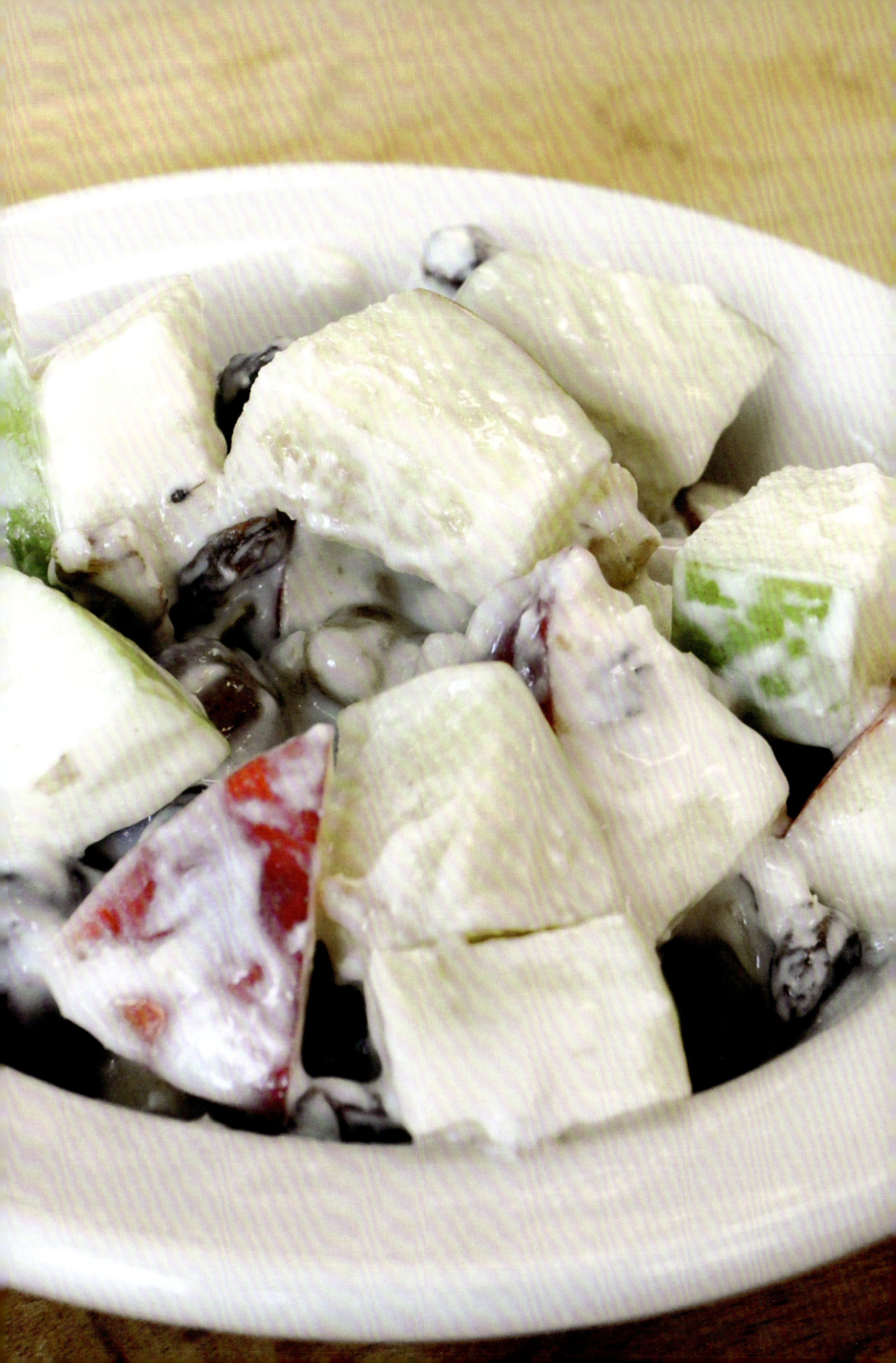

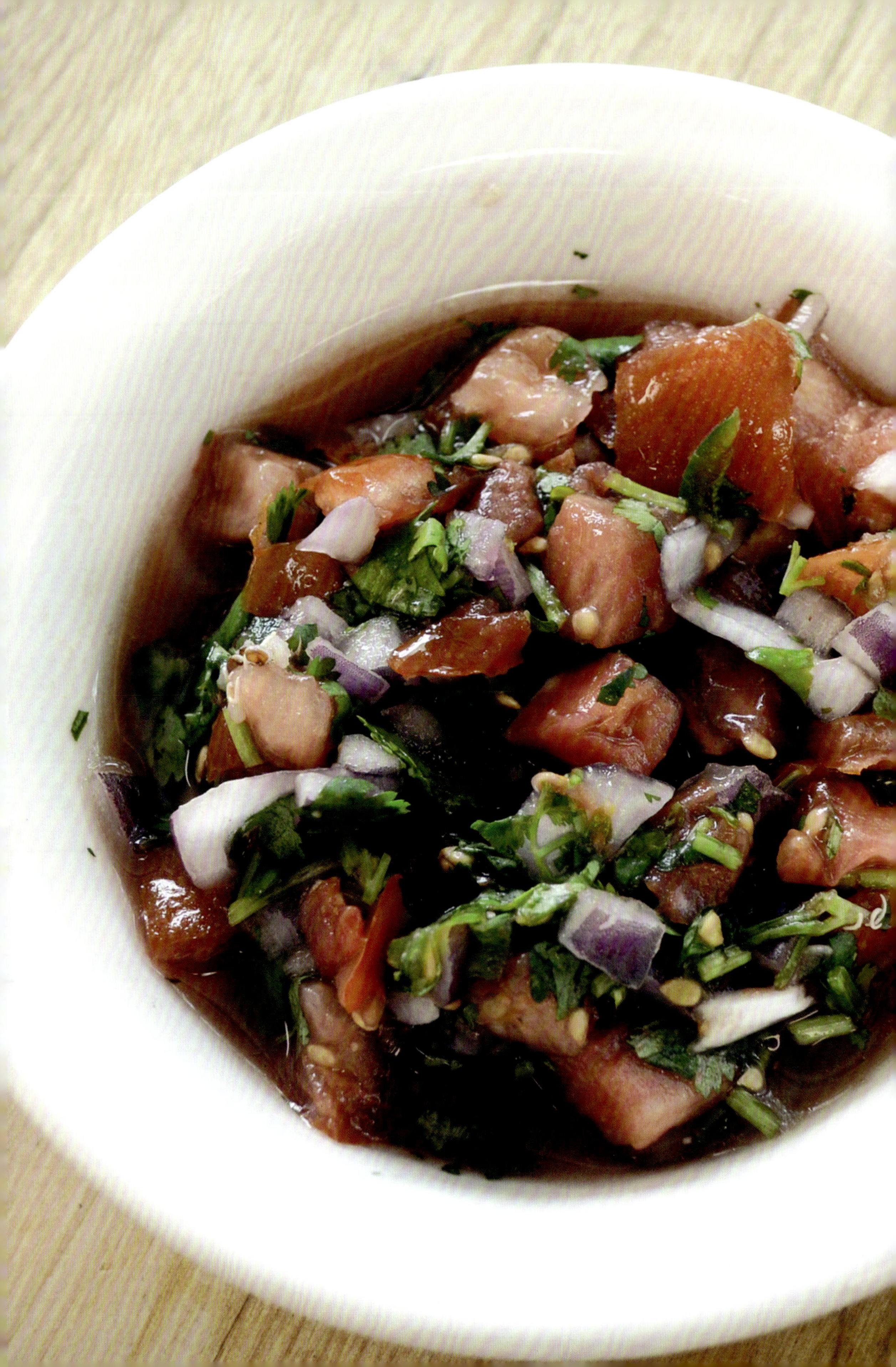

Use this wonderful tomato salsa as a starter with corn chips, or add it to the Mexican tuna salad for a complete meal (page 40).

Pico de Gallo
TOMATOES, JALAPEÑO, ONION

Core and chop the tomatoes. Chop the jalapeño, onion, and cilantro. Prepare a half cup of fresh lemon juice. Combine all ingredients. Serve immediately or refrigerate in an airtight container.

4 tomatoes, chopped
½ of a jalapeño, chopped
½ of an onion, chopped
A bunch of cilantro, chopped
½ cup lemon juice
Salt and pepper, to taste

Enjoy this traditional guacamole with corn tortilla chips as a starter, or as a side dish with baked fish or chicken.

Spicy Guacamole
AVOCADO, JALAPEÑO, CAYENNE PEPPER

4 - 5 ripe Hass avocados, pitted and peeled
½ red onion
2 medium tomatoes
1 jalapeño
½ bunch of cilantro
½ - 1 cup lemon juice
Sea salt, to taste
Cayenne pepper, to taste

Place all ingredients, except for one avocado, in a food processor. Pulse the ingredients until relatively smooth. Chop the remaining avocado and mash with a potato masher. Stir it into the guacamole. Serve immediately with corn tortilla chips, or as a topping on baked fish or chicken. Refrigerate leftover guacamole and store in an airtight container.

"If your diet is wrong, your medicine will not work, if your diet is right, your medicine is not needed."

- *Ayurvedic proverb*

Aside from being the oldest grain known to man, quinoa has tremendous health benefits. As a complete protein, quinoa provides lasting energy free from animal fats and gluten. Additionally, cooked quinoa contains a plethora of vitamins and minerals. Eat it alone or as a filling side to accompany any healthy meal.

A favorite of our customers at Food and Thought, this quinoa salad is packed with protein and flavor.

Hazelnut Feta Quinoa Salad
FETA AND CURRANTS

Boil the water on your stove top in a small or medium sauce pan. Add in both red and white quinoa and simmer for 15-20 minutes. While you are simmering the quinoa, soak the currants in a cup of water for 10-15 minutes, then drain. Remove the cooked quinoa from the heat, and let it sit for a few minutes to fluff. Toast the hazelnuts in the oven at 350 degrees for about 7-8 minutes. Combine all ingredients in one bowl, and stir to incorporate. Refrigerate the salad in an airtight container. Serve over fresh red leaf lettuce with chopped tomato, or use to accompany chicken or fish.

1¼ cup water
½ cup red quinoa
½ cup white quinoa
¼ cup toasted hazelnuts, chopped
¼ cup currants
1 bunch green onions, chopped
8 ounces crumbled feta
¼ cup red wine vinegar
¼ cup olive oil
Salt and pepper, to taste

Salads

Make this salad with the variety of organic potatoes of your choice. Serve the salad with our humm-burger (page 107), or on top of mixed greens.

Potato Salad
MUSTARD, PAPRIKA, APPLE CIDER VINEGAR

6 potatoes, boiled and peeled

1 cup mayonnaise

¼ cup red onion, chopped

¼ cup red pepper, chopped

¼ cup parsley, chopped

2 celery stalks, chopped

2 boiled eggs

2 tablespoons cucumber relish

1 tablespoon mustard

1 tablespoon apple cider vinegar

1 teaspoon dill

1 teaspoon paprika

Salt and pepper, to taste

Boil the potatoes over medium heat until cooked through, about 20 minutes. At the same time, hard boil the eggs in a small sauce pan. After the potatoes and eggs are done, peel them. Chop the cooked potatoes and the eggs, and combine them with all other ingredients in a large bowl. Serve with a parsley garnish, or refrigerate and store in an airtight container.

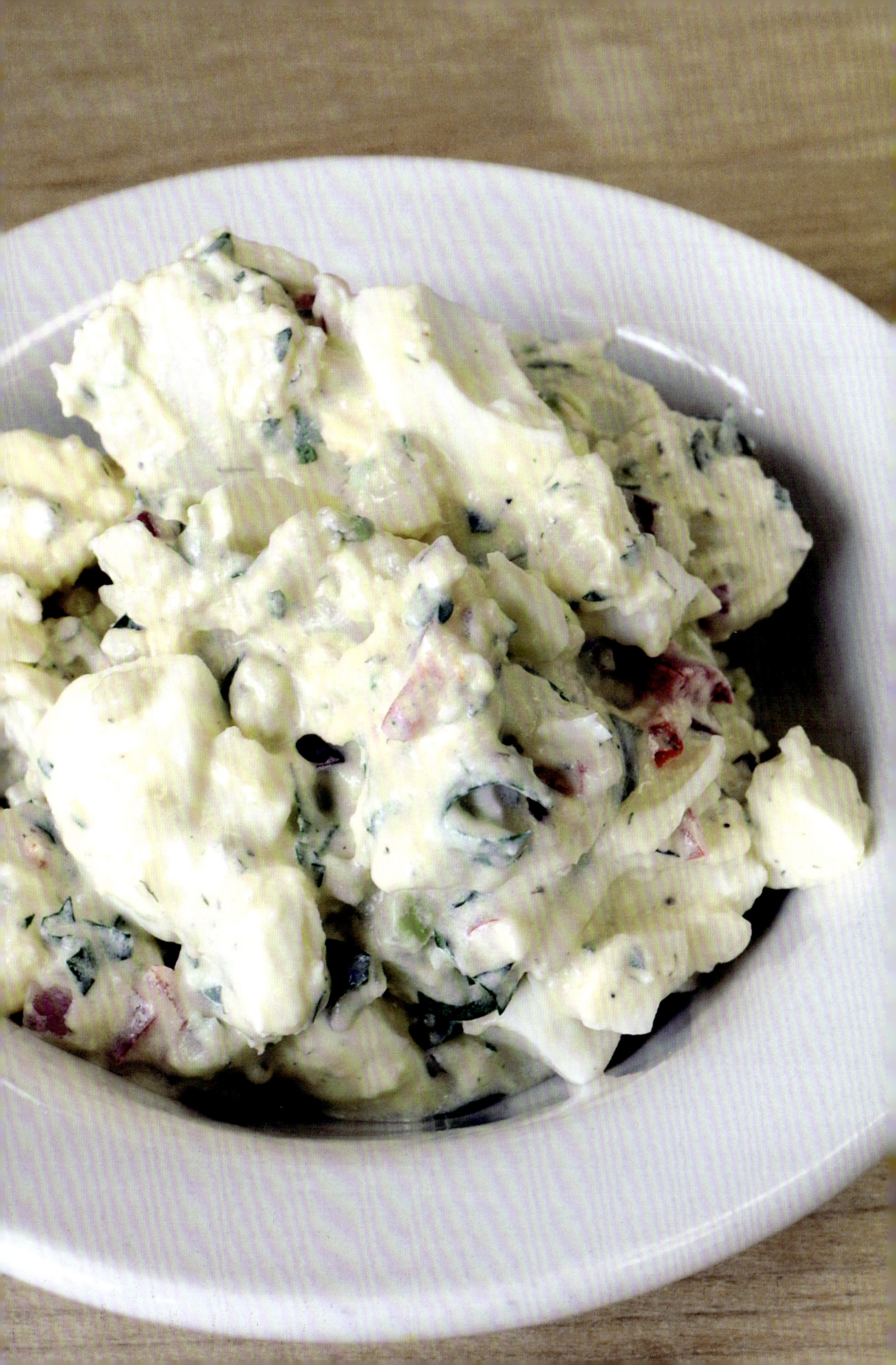

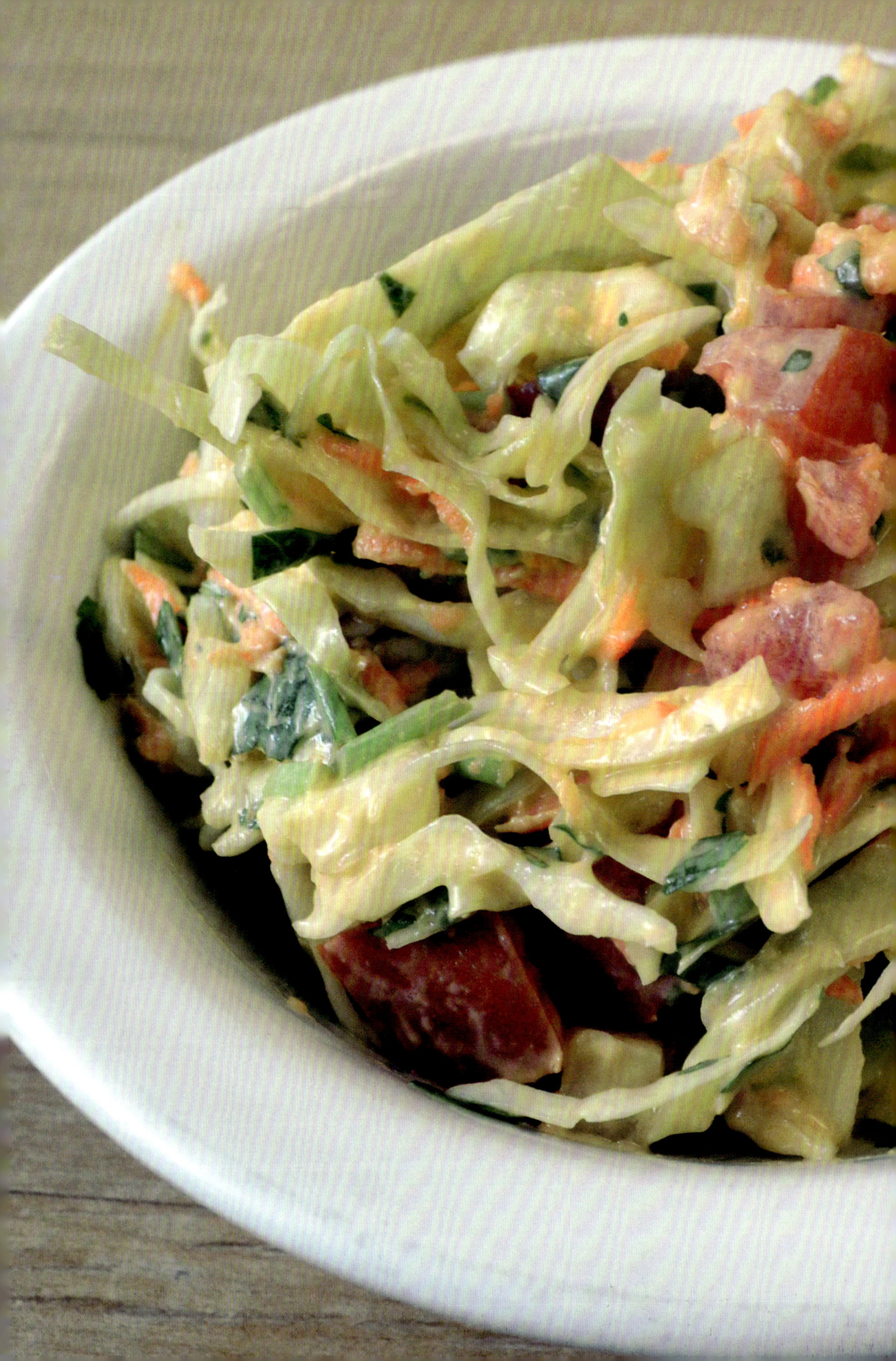

This cole slaw variation is great as a side dish or as an accoutrement on top of a grilled burger or grilled chicken sandwich. Combine with pico de gallo (page 49) and use as a filling for a lunch time spelt wrap.

Costa Rican Cole Slaw
GREEN CABBAGE, JALAPEÑO, LEMON JUICE

Prepare all ingredients as specified, and combine in a large bowl. Refrigerate in an airtight container, or serve immediately.

½ of a green cabbage, sliced thinly
1 tomato, chopped
½ of a jalapeño, chopped
½ of a red onion, chopped
2 carrots, shredded
½ bunch cilantro, chopped fine
1 cup vegannaise
½ cup lemon juice
Salt and pepper, to taste

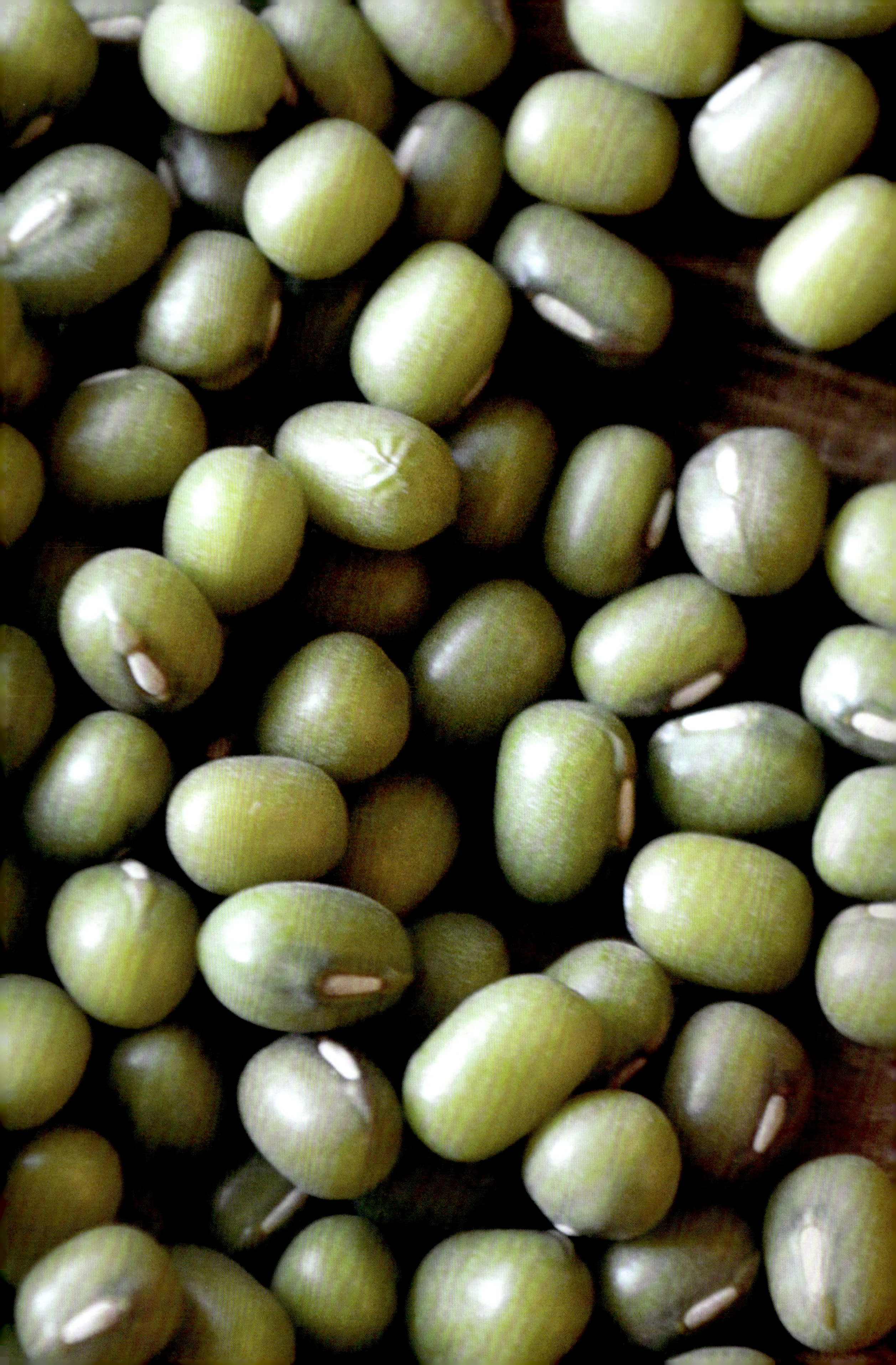

SOUPS

Everyday at Food and Thought, we serve two varieties of organic, freshly made soup during lunch and dinner. These soups are very popular coupled with a sandwich from our cold bar, a fresh pressed juice from our juice bar, or a plate of our simple sides. Make these soups for your family as an accompaniment to any meal or as the main dish.

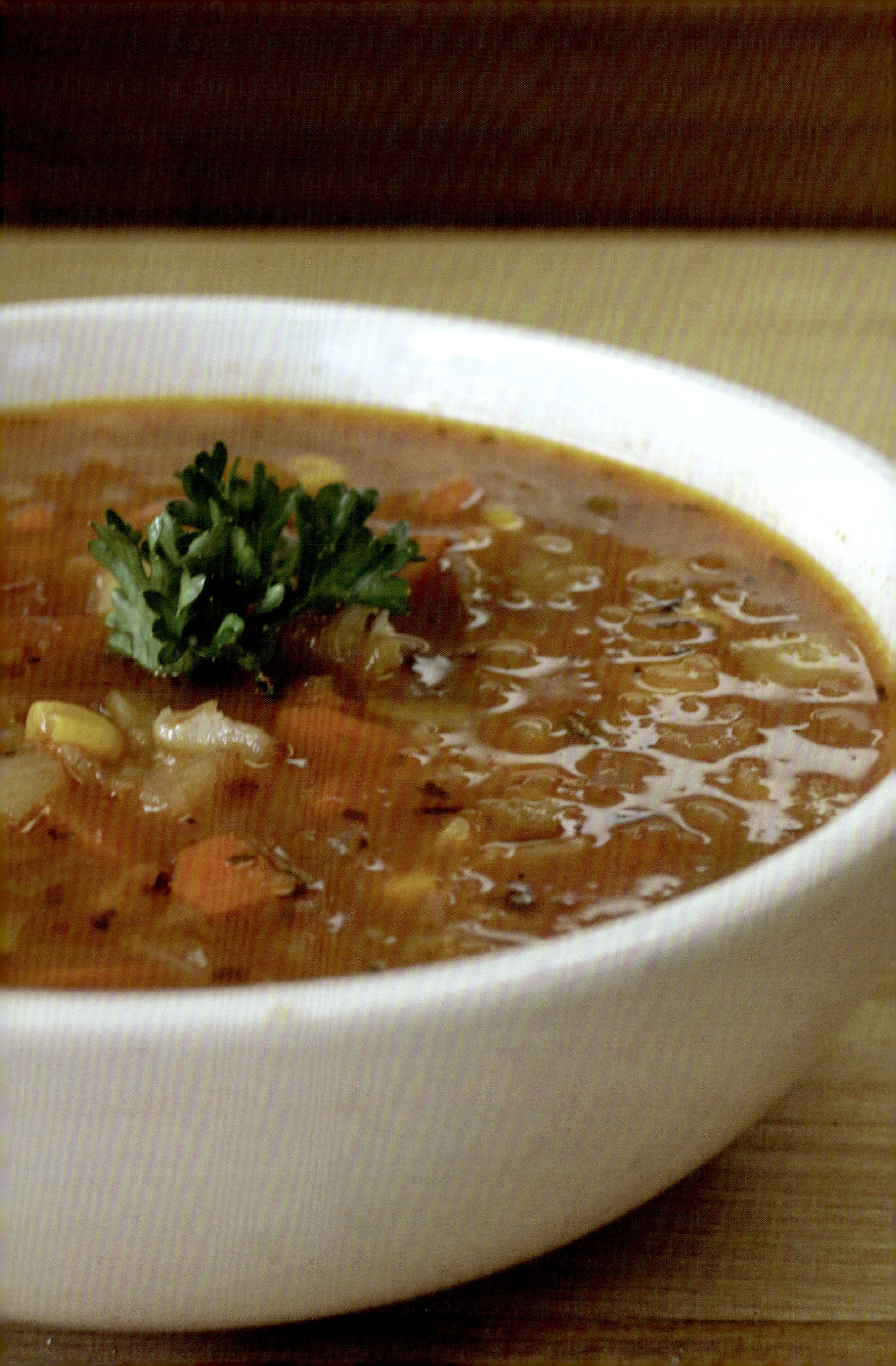

This was Frank's favorite vegetable soup. It's filled with a variety of vegetables and herbs.

Delaware Vegetable Soup
TOMATO, GREEN BEANS, CARROTS

Bring vegetable broth to a boil. Add in the potatoes, turnips, parsnips and carrots. Let simmer for 15 minutes, then add in the remaining vegetables. Cook until vegetables are soft. Add in spices, seasonings, and sauces then simmer for an additional 10 min.

2 quarts vegetable broth

2 bay leaves

1/2 cup chopped turnips or parsnips

2 carrots, chopped

¼ cup celery, chopped

¼ cup onion, chopped

2 potatoes

¼ cup corn

½ cup green beans

1 cup tomatoes, chopped

16 oz can tomato sauce

2 tablespoon tomato paste

¼ cup parsley, finely chopped

½ teaspoon Italian seasoning

¼ teaspoon thyme

¼ teaspoon basil

Pinch of cayenne, sea salt, garlic, olive oil

This favorite can also be made with garbanzo beans for a delightful variation.

Lentil Stew
CARROTS, ONION, GARLIC

4 cups water

2 cups French or green lentils

2 bay leaves

8 red skin potatoes, chopped

4 carrots, diced

½ of an onion, puréed with 2 tomatoes

2 nutritional yeast

1 bunch cilantro, chopped

2 cloves minced garlic

1 tablespoon olive oil

1 teaspoon sea salt

Boil the water, and add in the lentils. As the lentils are cooking, sauté the minced garlic in a bit of olive oil. Set aside. After about 20 minutes (or when the lentils are almost done), add in all remaining ingredients, including the tomato-onion purée. Let everything simmer for 15-20 minutes.

Variation: Garbanzo Bean Stew – use the same recipe as above, but substitute garbanzo beans (soaked overnight) in place of the lentils. Cook the beans for about 35-45 minutes, then add in the remaining ingredients. Let everything simmer for 15-20 minutes.

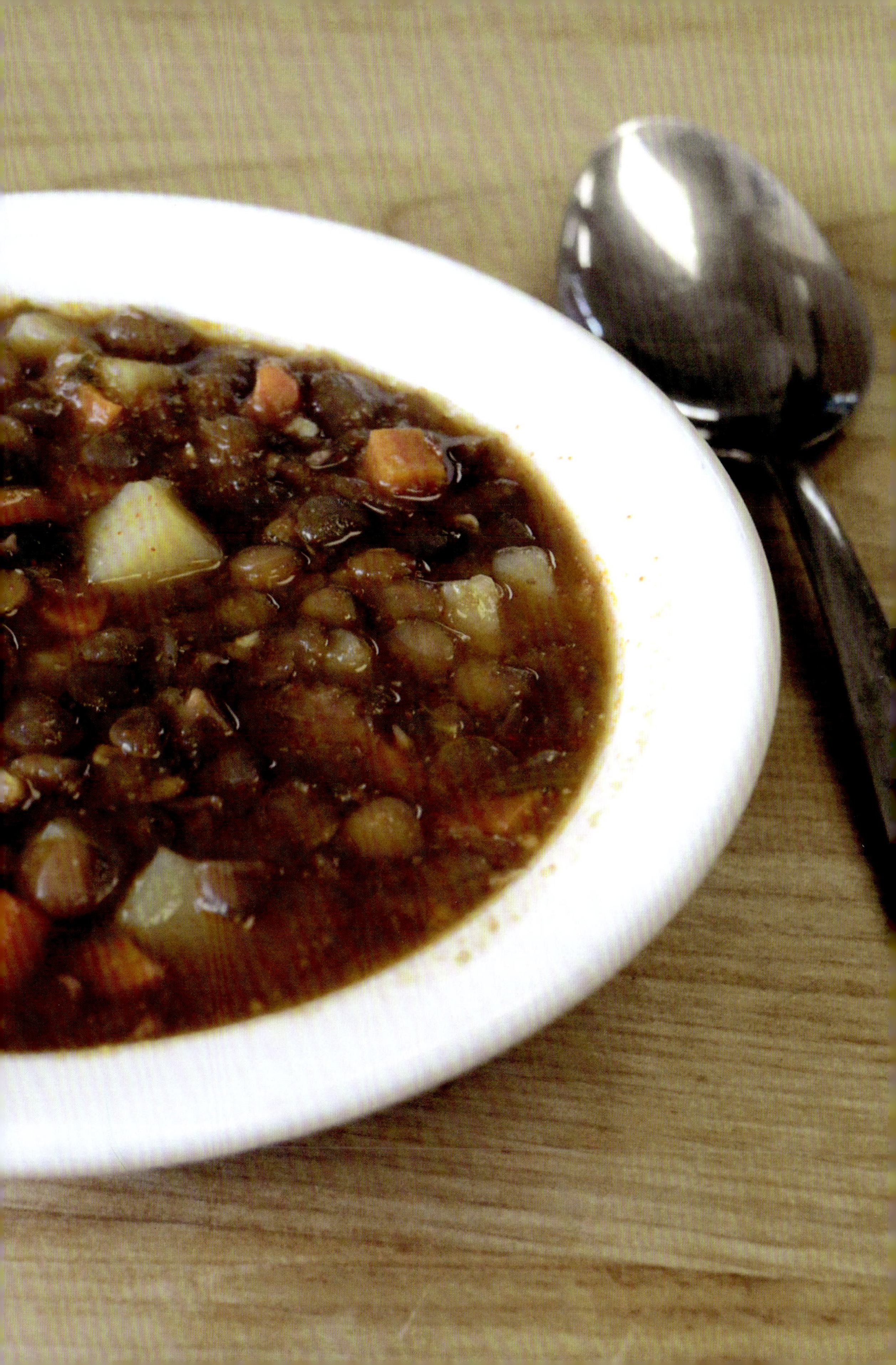

Rather than using canned red and black beans (pressure cooked) for this recipe, use freshly cooked beans that have been properly soaked. They are much healthier for the digestive system. Soak the beans overnight, then drain and rinse. Boil some water, and cook black beans and red beans (separately) at a simmer for about 35-40 minutes. Cooked beans may be stored in an airtight container in the refrigerator or frozen.

With properly soaked and freshly cooked beans, this is our twist on a traditional Italian favorite.

Minestrone
BLACK BEANS, CARROTS, RICE PASTA

Boil water. Add in remaining ingredients, except for the cooked rice pasta. Simmer for 20-25 minutes over medium low heat. Add in the cooked gluten-free pasta at the very end, prior to serving.

4 cups water

2 bay leaves

½ cup celery, chopped

4 cups carrots, chopped

2 cups baby spinach

1 cup cooked black beans

1 cup cooked red beans

½ cup frozen corn

14 ounces canned tomato purée

½ cup diced onion

2 cloves minced garlic

1 cup cooked gluten-free pasta, prepared as directed on the box (elbow, bow tie, or shells)

Sea salt, to taste

Soups

This is a great soup for a cloudy winter day when you need some comfort food! We make it at Food and Thought in the months following Christmas when the temperature drops in Southwest Florida.

Potato Leek Soup

LEEKS, BAY LEAVES, CORN

6 cups water

Red skin or Yukon potatoes, cut into chunks

2 bay leaves

2 - 3 stalks leeks, thinly sliced

1 cup cream

4 tablespoons butter

2 cloves minced garlic

½ teaspoon white pepper

½ teaspoon black pepper

Sea salt, to taste

1 cup corn (optional)

Boil the potatoes in the water with the bay leaves. Cook until the potatoes are soft, about 20 min. Sauté the leeks and garlic with butter in a seperate skillet. Add the prepared leeks (the more leeks, the better, in our opinion), cream, and seasonings. Add in the corn. Simmer for an additional 5-10 minutes.

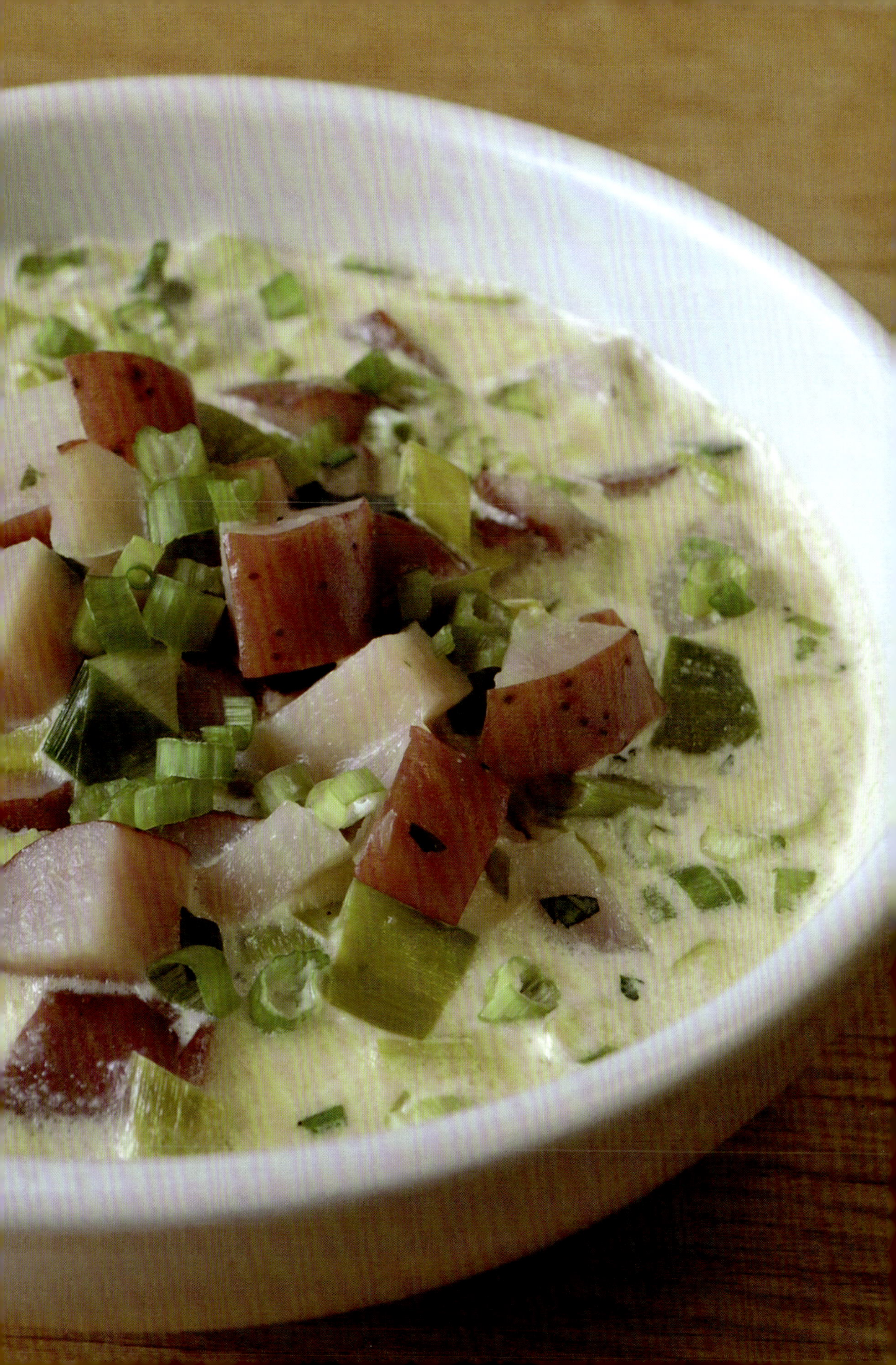

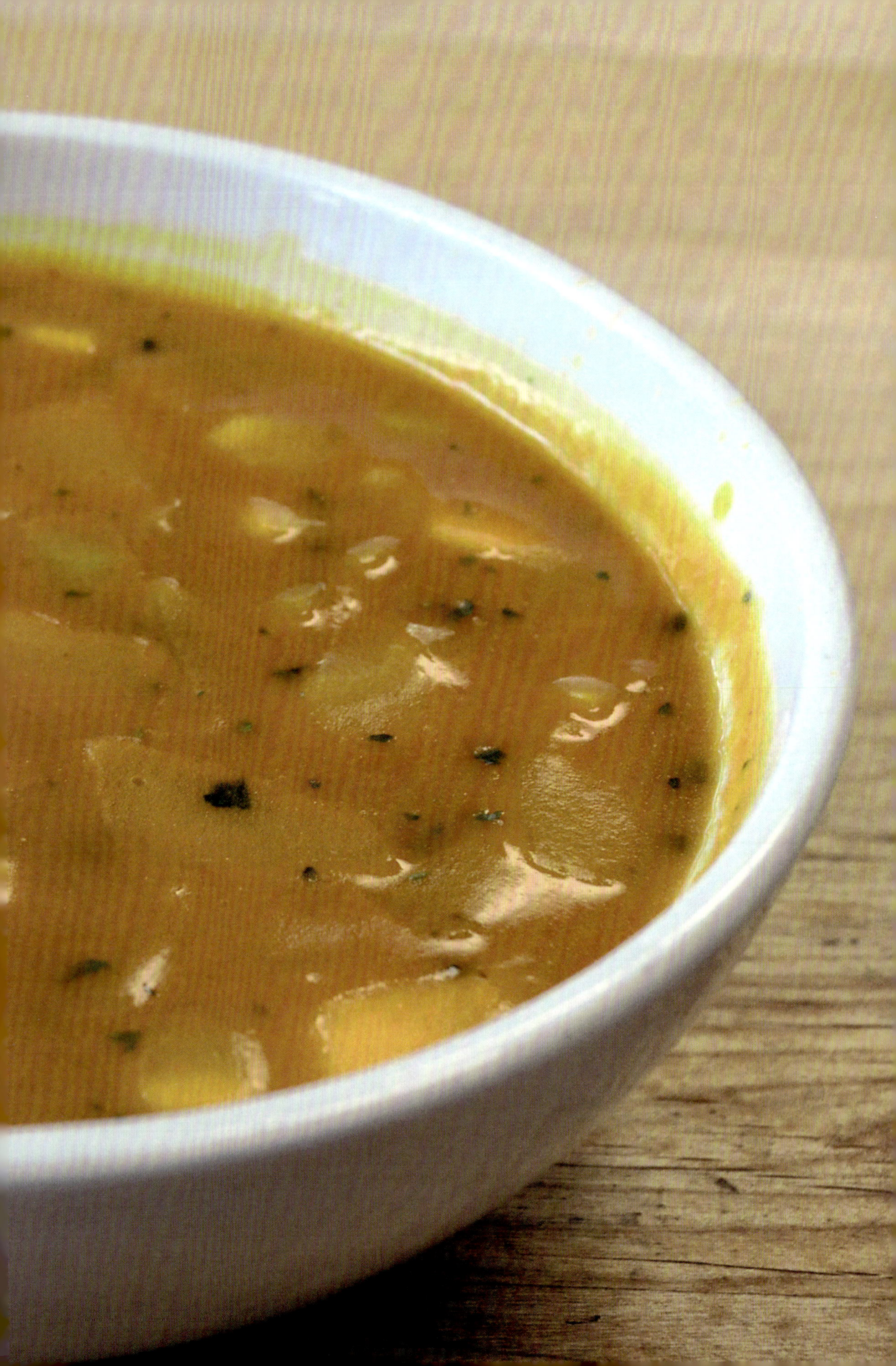

This creamy, delicious soup is very popular. The flavors are specific to autumn, when pumpkins are abundant. This recipe calls for three pumpkins, and when we make our soup, we aren't picky about what type of pumpkins we use. You can use whatever type you like – you can even try it with butternut squash.

Pumpkin Soup

PUMPKIN, NUTMEG, CINNAMON

Peel, cut, and seed three pumpkins. Steam the pieces for 20-25 minutes on the stove top over medium heat. Purée 2/3rds of the steamed pumpkins in a blender. Chop the remaining steamed pumpkin pieces into even smaller pieces. Place the purée and pumpkin pieces in a large pot, along with the remaining ingredients. Simmer lightly to let the flavors seep in for 10-15 min.

- 3 small pumpkins
- ¼ cup agave nectar
- 4 tablespoons butter
- 1 teaspoon dried cilantro leaves
- A pinch or two of nutmeg
- A pinch of cinnamon
- Sea salt, to taste

Soups

Stop by Food and Thought on Fridays during winter and spring for turkey rice soup - or make some at home for your family.

Turkey Rice Soup

CARROTS, BROWN RICE, PEAS

4 cups water

2 bay leaves

2 cups diced carrots

1 cup chopped celery and 1 cup chopped onion (sautéed together)

2T butter

1 bunch curly or Italian parsley chopped

4 cups chopped turkey meat (dark or light)

½ cup cream

1 cup brown rice, cooked

1 cup corn

1 cup peas

Salt and pepper, to taste

Garlic, to taste

Sauté the chopped celery and onion together for a bit (approximately 5-7 minutes) in the butter. Bring the water to a boil; add the bay leaves, diced carrots, celery, onion, parsley and meat. Simmer the mixture for 15-20 minutes. Add the remaining ingredients, and simmer for an additional 10-15 minutes.

As our tribute to the holiday season and lovely, cooler winter weather, every Thursday is "Turkey Day." We bake turkeys in our oven and make creamy mashed potatoes and fresh stuffing. Because of the leftover turkey meat we inevitably have, Friday has unofficially become "Turkey Rice Soup Day."

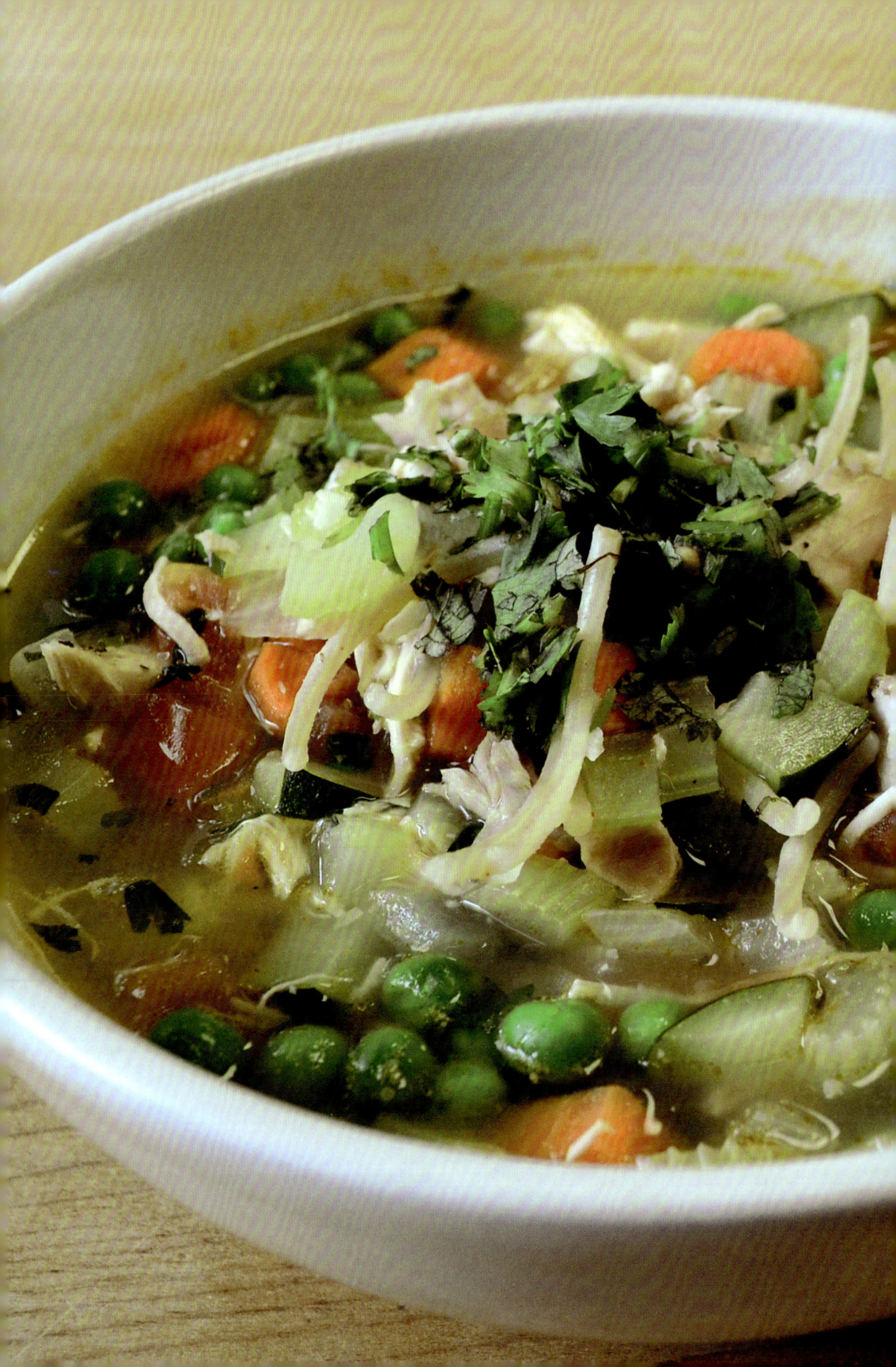

Our traditional chicken noodle soup is gluten-free when made with rice noodles. Delicious flavors can be customized based on the fresh herbs you have on hand.

Chicken Noodle Soup
CHICKEN, PEAS, BROWN RICE SPAGHETTI NOODLES

Cook one whole chicken by covering it with water and bringing to a boil. Cook over medium heat for 20-25 minutes. Pull out the chicken, and use the broth as a base for your soup. Debone and cut up chicken meat. Add it to the broth. Add in zucchini, carrots, onions, celery, peas, and cilantro, along with all seasonings and fresh herbs. Simmer everything together for 20-25 minutes. Add in prepared brown rice spaghetti noodles at the very end before serving.

4 cups chicken broth, made from a whole chicken
2 cups chopped green zucchini
1 cup chopped carrots
1 cup chopped onion
1 cup chopped celery
1 cup green peas
¼ cup chopped cilantro
1 cup brown rice spaghetti noodles, cooked
2 bay leaves
1 teaspoon garlic powder or minced garlic
1 teaspoon paprika
Salt and pepper, to taste
Any fresh herbs you have on hand (mint, thyme, oregano, basil)

Soups

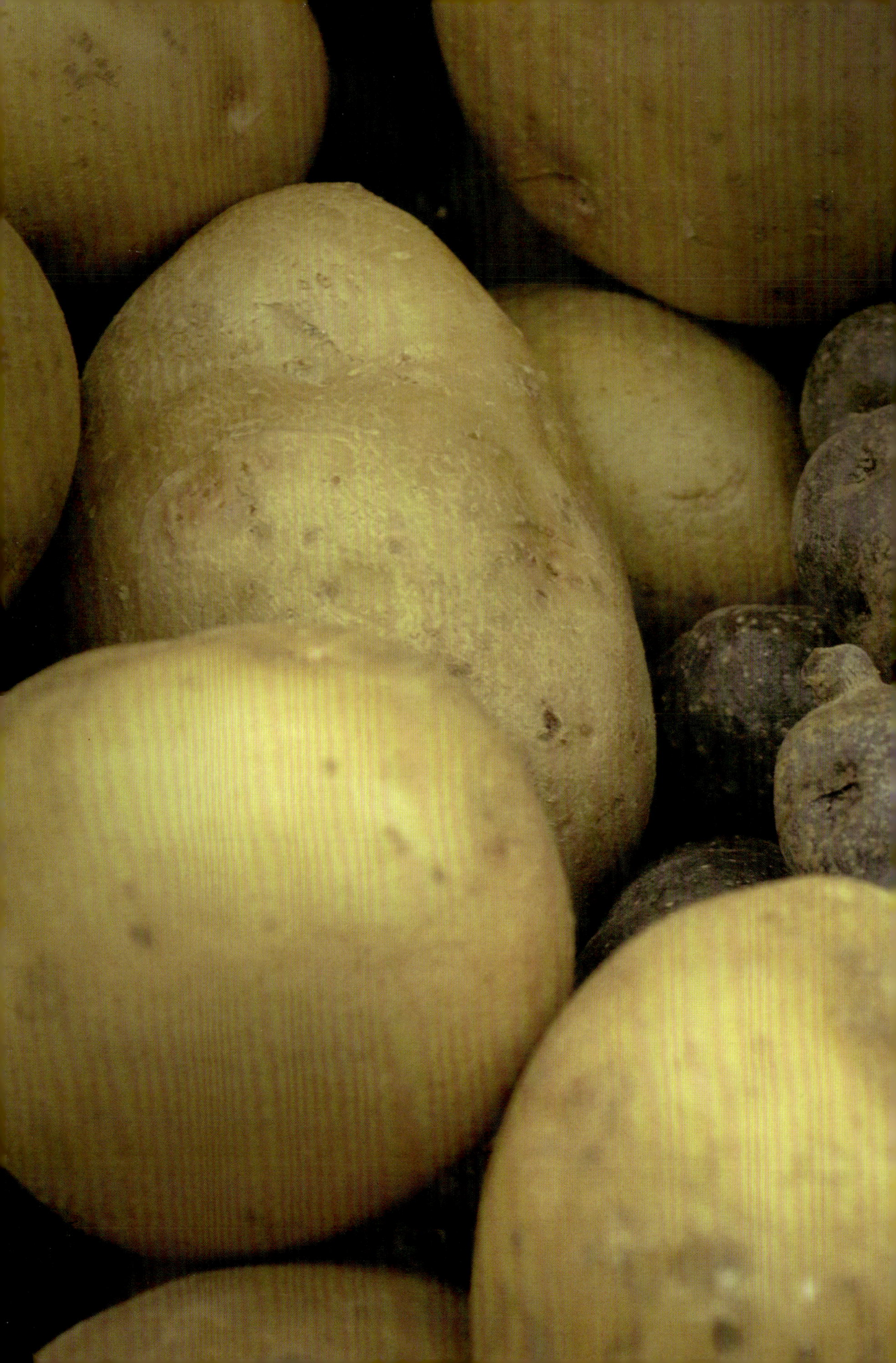

SIMPLE SIDES

The side dishes we serve each day at Food and Thought are simple - they are made to complement any of our entrees. As an added bonus, they are easy to prepare at home. Pair any main dish with any one or two of these side dishes for a complete meal.

" Let your food be your medicine, let your medicine be your food. "

- Hippocrates

The greens at Food and Thought are always the first to go during lunch and dinner, they are so popular! Replicating our steamed greens at home is so simple – this recipe can be easily modified based upon the greens currently in season.

Steamed Greens
COLLARD, KALE, SPINACH, OR CHARD

In a large pot, sauté the garlic in the olive oil. Add all remaining ingredients to the pot. Cook for 5-6 minutes on low, covered. Enjoy!

- 2 bunches of greens – collard, kale, spinach, or chard
- 1 whole onion, thinly sliced (optional)
- 1 whole tomato, thinly sliced (optional)
- 2 tablespoons olive oil
- 1 teaspoon garlic, chopped
- Sea salt, to taste

Our veggie sauté at Food and Thought is a crowd pleaser. Making it at home is very simple. Come to our market to grab a few fresh vegetables before making dinner.

Veggie Sauté
BROCCOLI, CABBAGE, CARROTS

3 - 4 vegetables, chopped
    or thinly sliced
- broccoli (florets)
- carrots
- yellow squash
- zucchini
- red onion
- red bell pepper
- cabbage
- cauliflower (florets)

2 - 3 tablespoons olive oil
1 teaspoon minced garlic
Salt and pepper, to taste

Sauté the garlic in the olive oil in a large skillet over medium heat. Throw on veggies, along with the salt and pepper. Put a lid on the skillet, and allow the vegetables to cook for 5-6 minutes (al dente) or 10-12 minutes (well done), stirring occasionally. Serve on the side of your main dish.

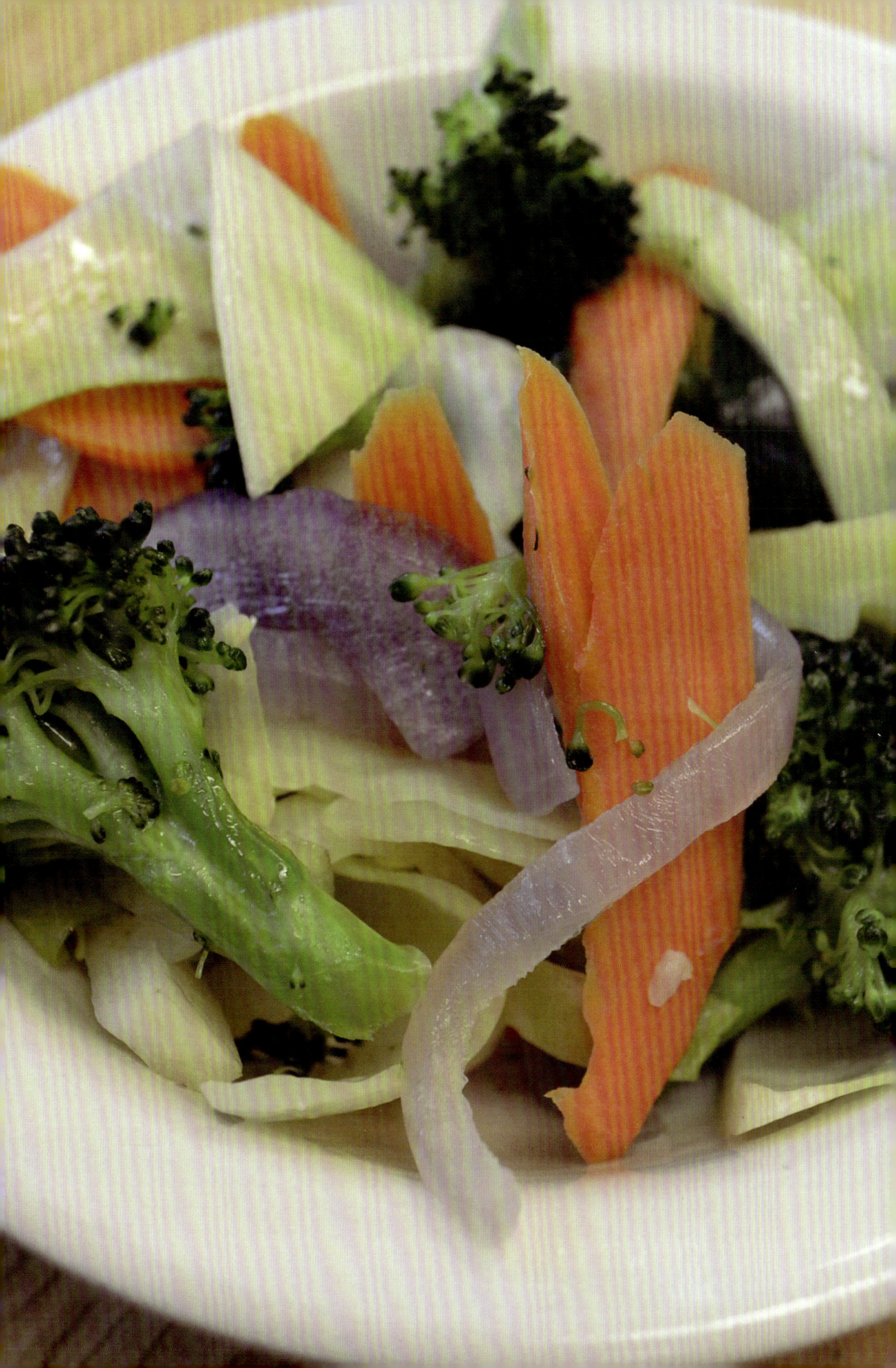

" Prayer in deed is good, but while calling on God, a man should himself lend a hand "

- *Hippocrates*

Serve our mashed potatoes with turkey Salisbury steak and gravy (pages 129-130) for a satisfying and rich meal. These simple potatoes taste great every time they are prepared!

Mashed Potatoes
POTATOES, HEAVY WHIPPING CREAM, GARLIC

Preheat the oven to 350 degrees. Roast the garlic in the oven for 5-10 minutes. Peel the potatoes, and then boil them for 20-25 minutes. Drain the water, then mash the potatoes. Add in the butter, cream, milk, salt, pepper, and roasted garlic. Beat the mixture, then serve with gravy. Garnish with fresh parsley.

4 potatoes
1 cup milk
½ stick butter
¼ cup heavy whipping cream
1 - 2 cloves roasted garlic
Salt and pepper, to taste
A few sprigs of fresh parsley (garnish)

Simple Sides

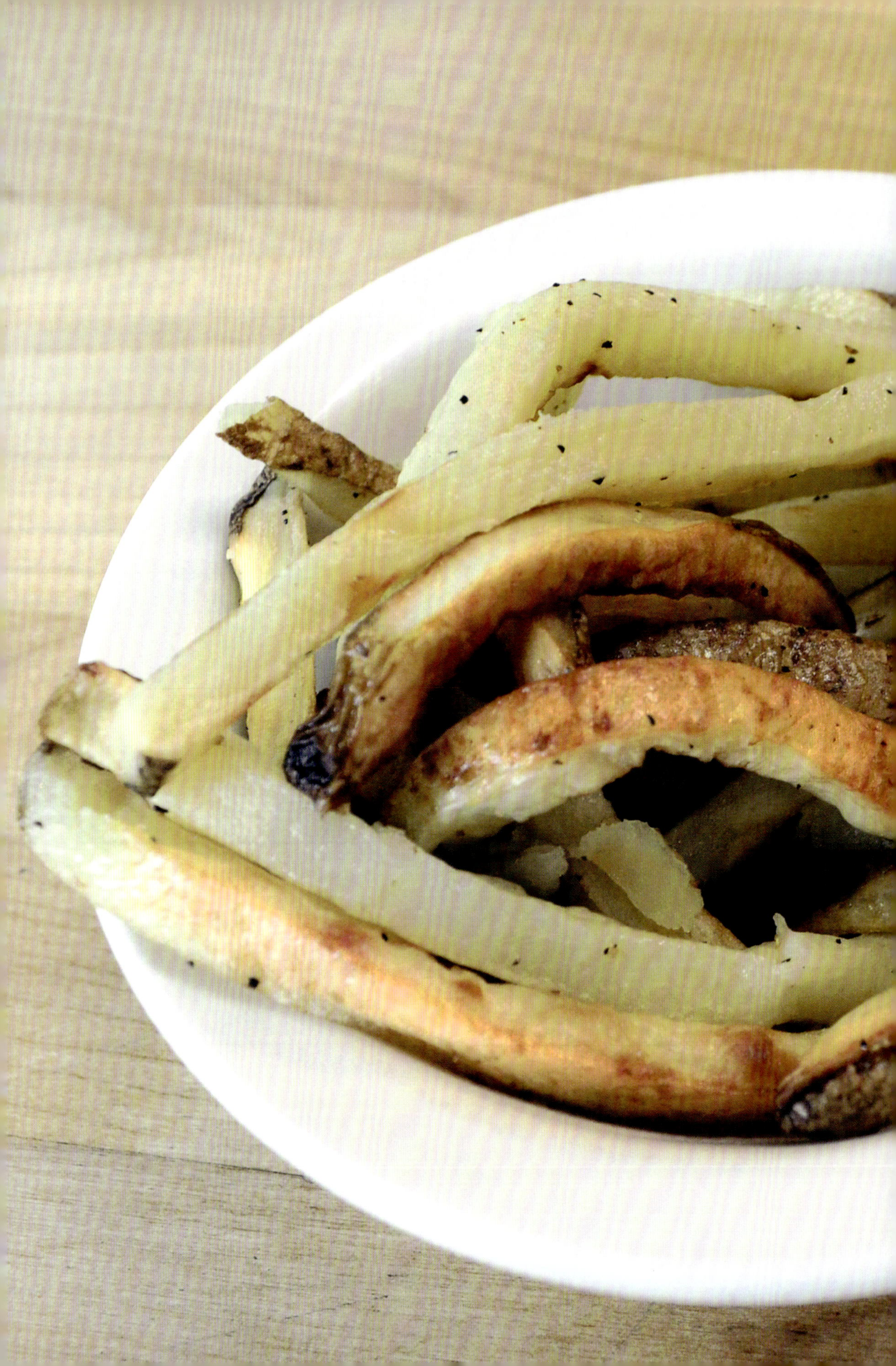

Named for Freedom Teague, head chef and author of this cookbook, our Freedom Fries are a delicious and special side dish. We don't serve them every day, but when we do, they are met with exclamations of delight.

Freedom Fries
YUKON GOLD POTATOES, SEA SALT, OLIVE OIL

Preheat the oven to 325 degrees. Slice the potatoes very thinly, like French fries. Toss them with olive oil, salt, and black pepper. Bake them on a cookie sheet for 25-30 minutes. Toss them intermittently, and bake a bit longer for crunchier fries. Serve immediately.

- 6 - 8 Russet or Yukon gold potatoes
- Olive oil
- Sea Salt
- Black Pepper

Simple Sides

These delicious patties are sweet, rich, and filling. They are a perfect addition to any meal and pair particularly well with a fresh baby greens salad.

Sweet Potato Patties
CINNAMON AND MAPLE SYRUP

4 or 5 sweet potatoes (3 cups mashed)

1 egg

1 cup white unbleached flour

¼ cup maple syrup

1 teaspoon cinnamon

Palm shortening for frying

Preheat your oven to 350 degrees. Bake the sweet potatoes for 35-40 minutes. Peel and mash the sweet potatoes. Add in the egg, maple syrup, flour, and cinnamon. Mix together until incorporated. Form the mixture into small patties the size of your palm, or use an ice cream scoop. Fry each patty in organic palm shortening. Turn each patty once; fry 3-4 minutes per side. Serve immediately, and garnish with maple syrup.

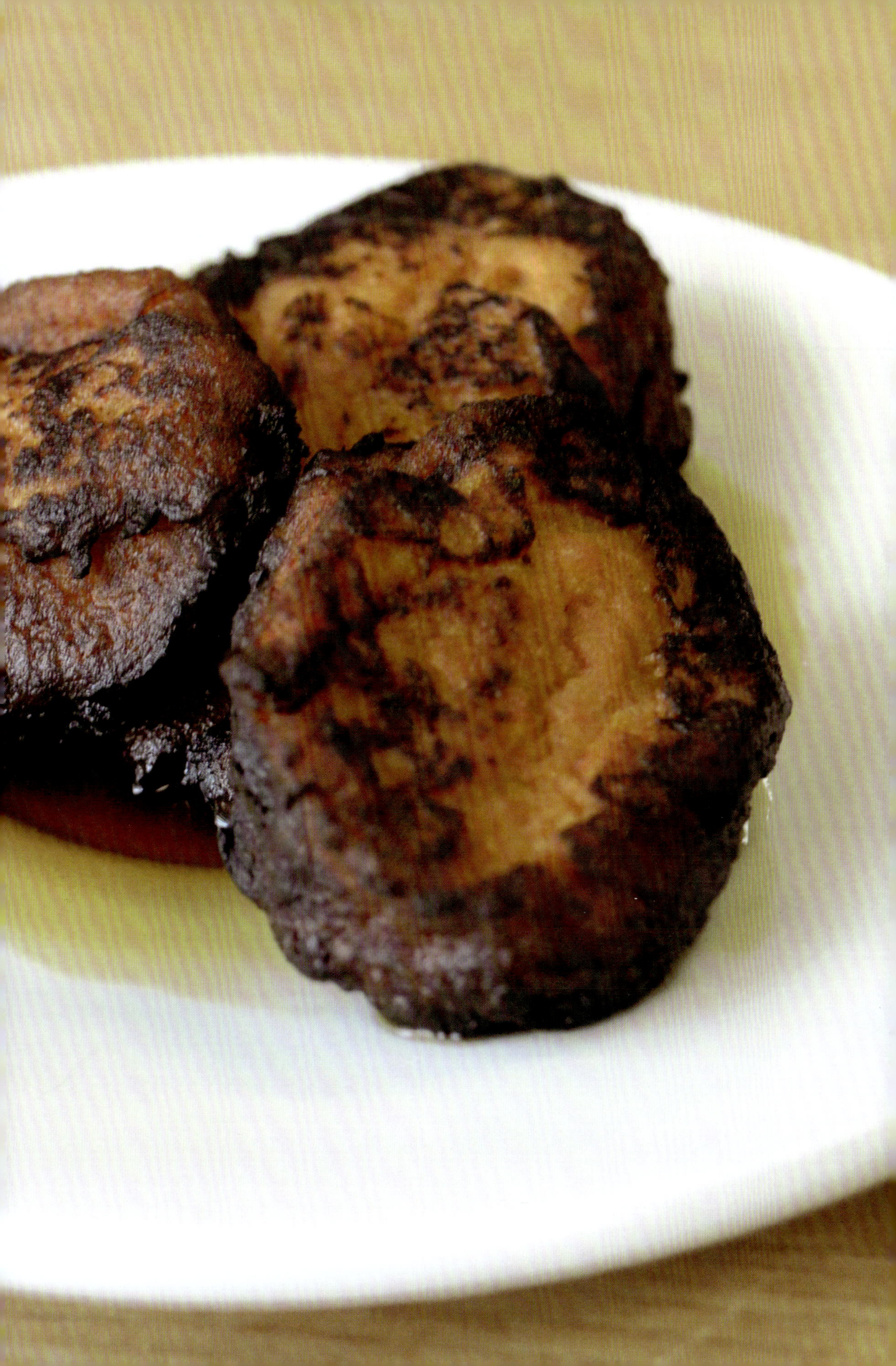

Every day, we serve some variation of brown rice. Using brown rice to complement a meal adds fiber and complex carbohydrates. Dress up plain brown rice by preparing this coconut version.

Coconut Brown Rice
BASMATI RICE, COCONUT MILK, GARLIC

1 cup brown basmati rice
1 cup water
1 cup coconut milk
¼ cup shredded coconut
¼ of an onion, chopped fine
2 tablespoons coconut oil
1 teaspoon minced garlic
½ teaspoon salt

In a medium sized pot, sauté the onion and minced garlic in coconut oil. After several minutes, add in the rice and continue to sauté until the rice begins to make a popping noise. Add in the water and coconut milk, along with a ½ teaspoon of salt and ¼ cup of shredded coconut. Bring the mixture to a boil, and then lower to a simmer. Place the lid on the pot, and then simmer for 25-30 minutes.

Always choose brown rice; white rice is created through a process of boiling, bleaching, and drying, which is detrimental your system and creates digestion issues. Brown rice is more pure and doesn't contain any additives. When you prepare rice, there is no need to rinse it out. Doing so strips the rice of its vitamins and minerals.

" To do nothing is sometimes a good remedy "

- *Hippocrates*

Use leftover (or fresh) brown rice to fix this recipe and serve on the side of chicken or fish. Add some cut up baked chicken to the rice for a complete, one dish meal.

Veggie Brown Rice
ONIONS, CARROTS, SCRAMBLED EGG

Sauté all of the vegetables in 2 tablespoons of olive oil for several minutes. Add in the cooked brown rice and the scrambled egg. Stir the mixture, and season to taste with salt and soy sauce. Serve immediately.

2 cups brown rice, cooked

¼ cup onions, chopped fine

¼ cup celery, chopped fine

¼ cup carrots, chopped fine

¼ cup peas

¼ cup corn

¼ cup cabbage, chopped fine

2 tablespoons olive oil

½ teaspoon sea salt

Soy sauce (optional)

1 scrambled egg (optional)

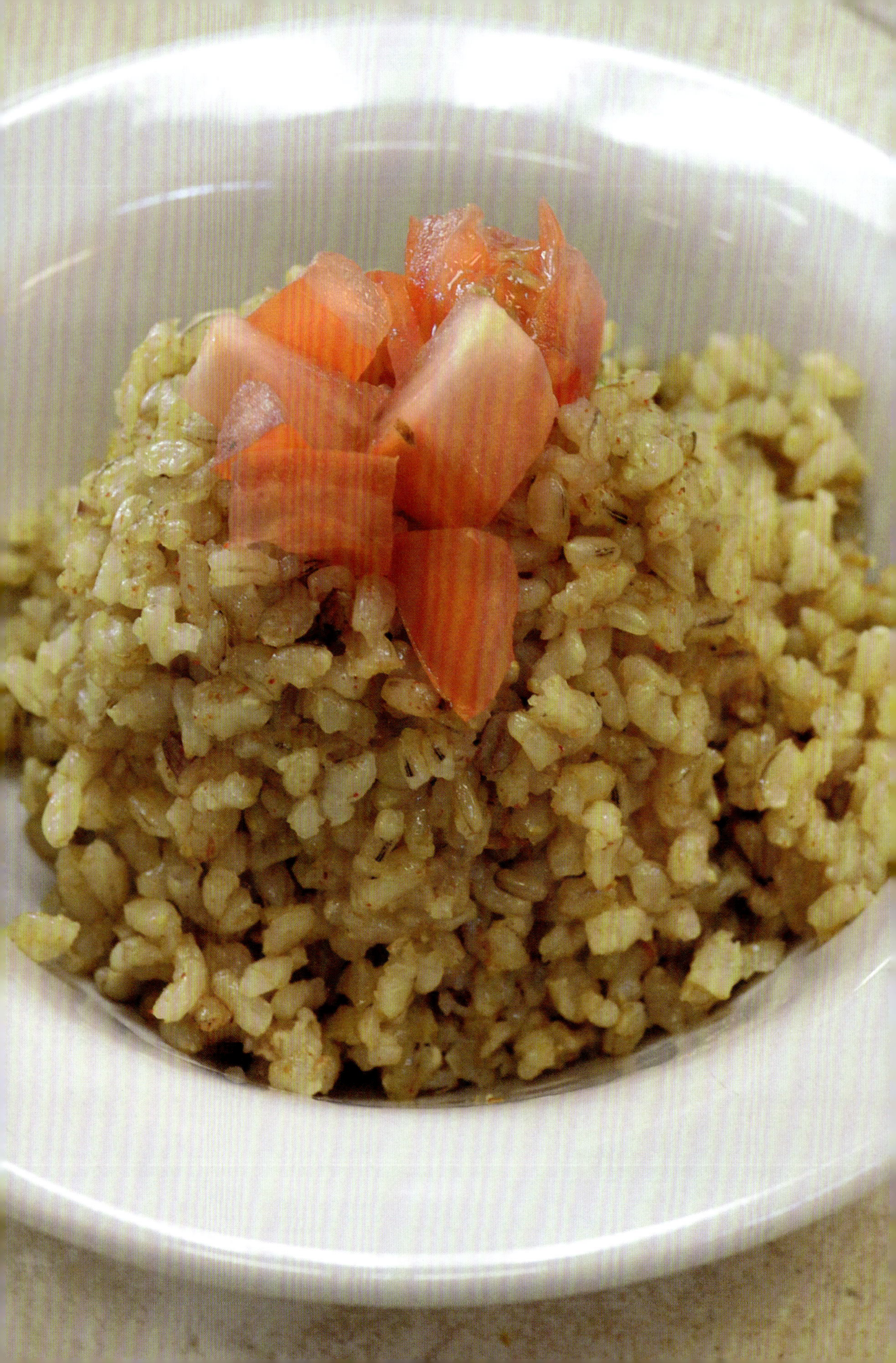

Another twist on brown rice, this dish is dressed up and flavorful.

Tomato Brown Rice
BROWN RICE, ONION, GARLIC

Sauté the onion and garlic in olive oil for several minutes. Add in the rice and sauté until the rice begins to make a popping noise. Add the tomato purée and water. Bring the mixture to a boil. Lower the heat, cover the pot, and let the mixture simmer for 25-30 minutes.

1 cup short grain brown rice
1¼ cup water
1 cup puréed tomato
¼ of an onion, chopped fine
2 tablespoons olive oil
1 teaspoon minced garlic

Whenever you make beans at home, the process and corresponding recipe will remain the same. The following directions apply for adzuki, lima, red kidney, pinto, and black turtle beans, as well as black eyed peas.

Beans
CILANTRO, GARLIC, SEA SALT

Beans
1 - 2 bay leaves
¼ - ½ of an onion, chopped
¼ - ½ bunch cilantro, chopped
Minced garlic, to taste
Paprika, to taste
Salt and pepper, to taste

Soak your beans overnight in a big pot filled with water. Make sure the water covers all of the beans. After soaking overnight, drain and rinse the beans. Refill the pot with water about an inch over the beans. Add a bay leaf or two. Bring the pot to a boil, then reduce the heat and simmer for 45 minutes. Add in seasonings, to taste – paprika, chopped onion, garlic, cilantro, sea salt, and/or black pepper. Simmer for an additional 10-15 minutes.

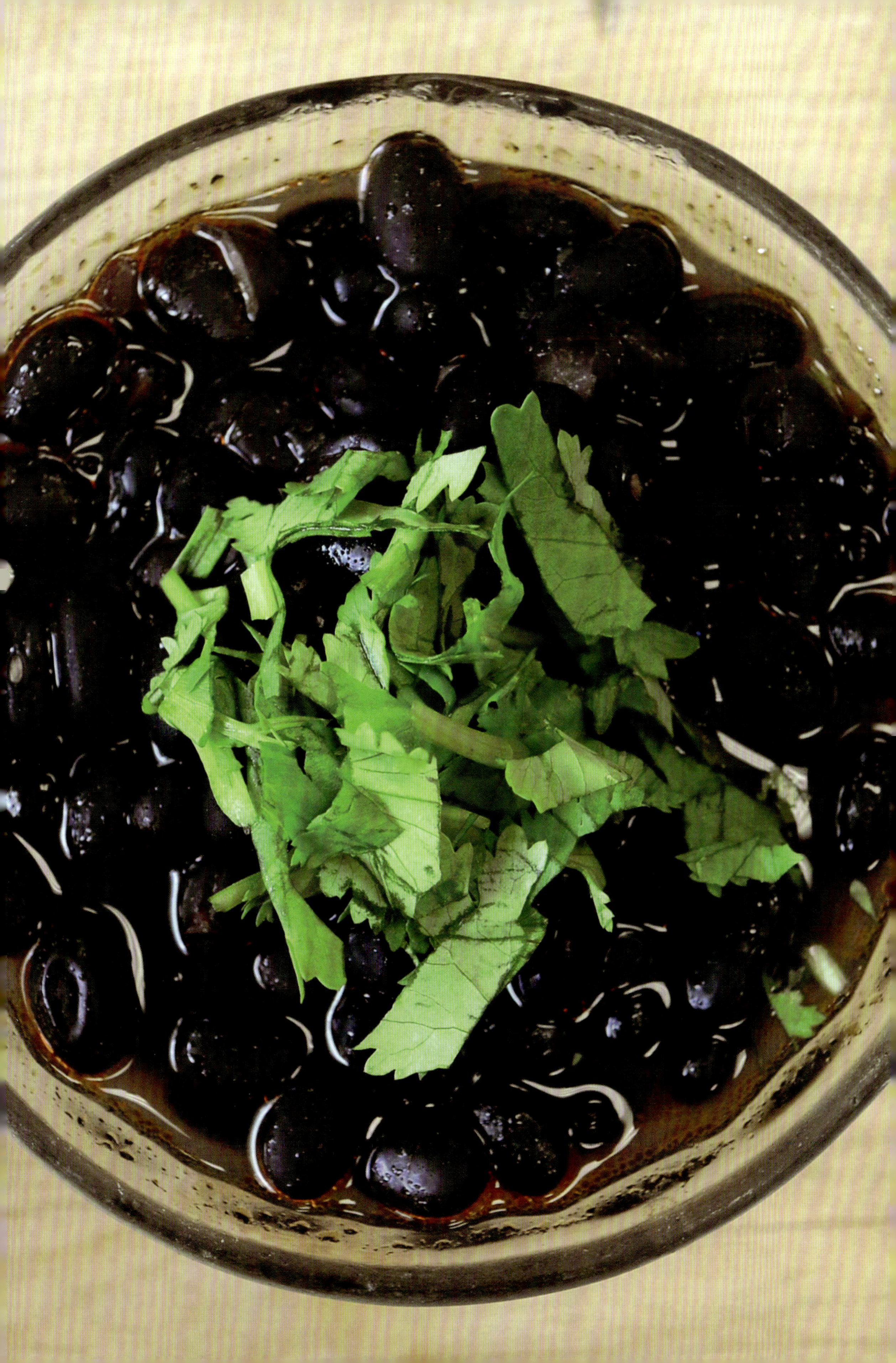

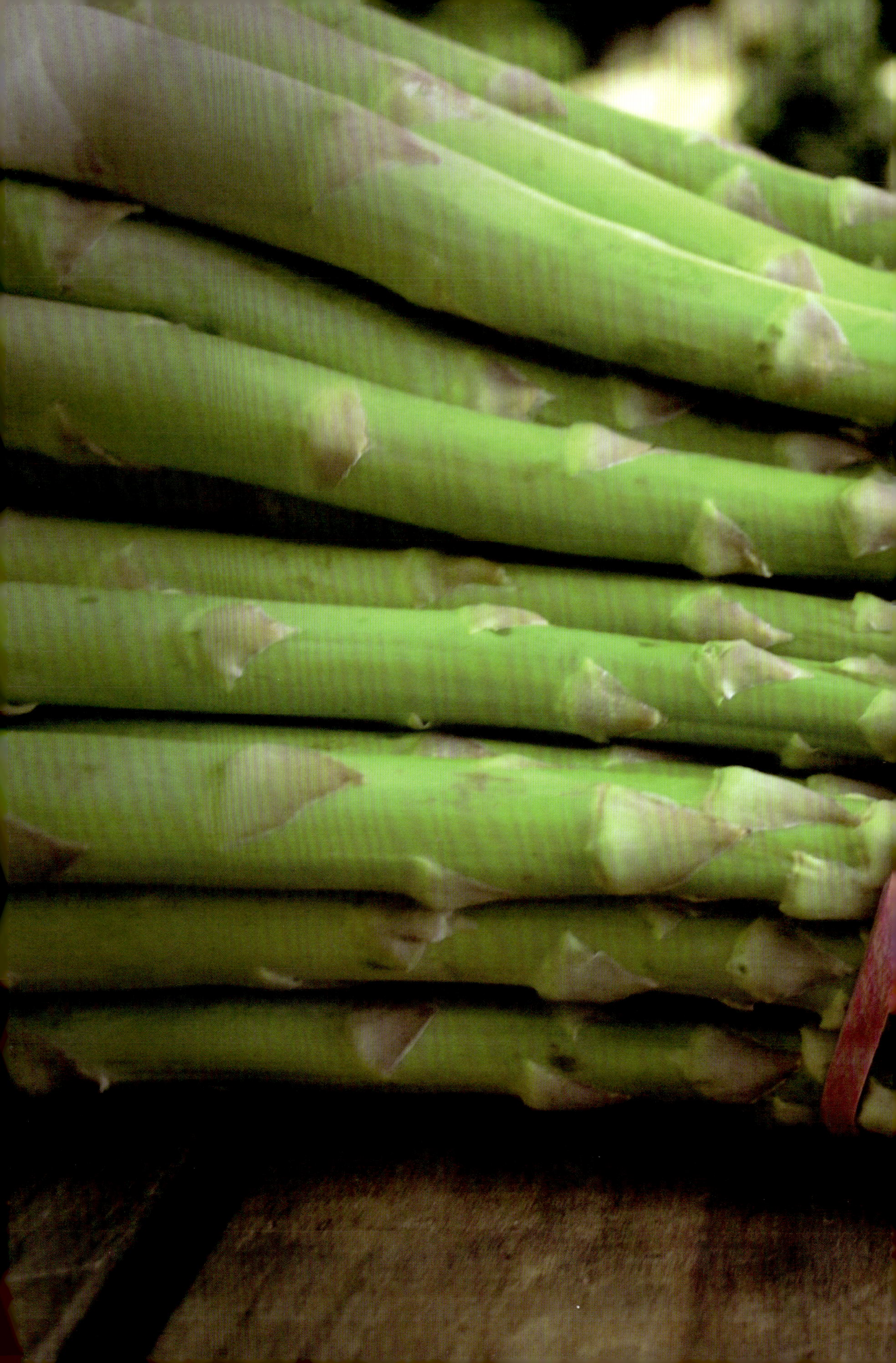

VEGETARIAN

We serve one vegetarian main course each day at Food & Thought. When you prepare these dishes at home, you'll notice that we use relatively few ingredients and a simple style of preparation, allowing the fresh food to speak for itself. Whether you consistently eat a vegetarian diet or not, these dishes are filling, simple, and delicious.

This recipe calls for sprouted wheat flour, making it a great choice for those looking to cut back on their gluten intake.

Zucchini Crusted Pizza
ZUCCHINI, SPINACH, BASIL

The Crust

4 - 5 zucchini, shredded

1 to 1½ cups sprouted wheat flour

1 egg

1 teaspoon sea salt

1 teaspoon oregano

Preheat the oven to 350 degrees. Mix the shredded zucchini together with a teaspoon of salt. Let the mixture sit for a few minutes. Place it in a pasta strainer to squeeze out the excess water. Add in an egg, the oregano, and the flour. Mix it all together. Press the crust mixture into two 9 inch cake pans. Bake the crust for 25 minutes, or until golden brown. Let it cool for about 10-15 minutes before adding the toppings.

The Toppings

Spread the can of pizza sauce over the top of your pizza crusts, along with the spinach. Cover the spinach leaves with the mozzarella cheese. Top the pizzas with the tomato, onion, peppers, and olives. (You can top the pizza with any vegetables your family enjoys). Sprinkle basil on top of both pizzas. Bake for 15 minutes at 350 degrees.

1 can of pizza sauce
1 box of baby spinach leaves
2 cups shredded mozzarella
1 tomato, chopped
¼ of an onion, chopped
Red, yellow, or orange bell peppers, chopped
½ cup olives
Basil

This lovely vegetarian dish tastes delicious and presents beautifully! It is a simple meal to make at home.

Eggplant Boats
EGGPLANT, BROWN RICE, MOZZARELLA

Preheat the oven to 350 degrees. Cut both eggplants in half, and scoop out the middle. Set the meat aside. Brush the insides of the eggplants with olive oil and bake in the oven for 20-25 minutes, or until golden. Chop up the vegetables, including the eggplant meat. Sauté the vegetables together in a few tablespoons of olive oil for 7-10 minutes. Stir the cooked rice in with the vegetable mixture. Fill the eggplant halves with the veggie rice mixture and sprinkle with mozzarella. Garnish each boat with a slice of tomato. Place the boats back in the oven for 10-12 minutes, or until the cheese is fully melted. Serve on a plate with a tomato sauce garnish.

2 eggplants
½ of a red onion, chopped
1 cup chopped peppers
1 cup chopped tomatoes
1 cup cooked brown rice
1 cup shredded mozzarella
Sliced tomato and tomato sauce, for garnish

This recipe is very simple, delicious, and gluten-free. It calls for a good amount of pesto sauce. You can choose to make pesto from scratch or purchase a container of freshly made, organic pesto in our store.

Italian Lasagna
RICE LASAGNA NOODLES AND RICOTTA CHEESE

- 1 box rice lasagna noodles, cooked per directions
- 1 can tomato sauce
- 1 container ricotta cheese
- 8 - 12 ounces Freedom's Pesto
- 16 ounces Italian cheese blend (parmesan, Romano, mozzarella, and provolone)
- 1 - 2 teaspoons Italian seasoning

Preheat the oven to 350 degrees. Cook the rice lasagna noodles per directions. Cool the noodles immediately in cold water to prevent the pasta from getting too mushy. Layer tomato sauce, noodles, ricotta, pesto, and shredded cheese (in that order) in a 9 by 13 inch baking dish. Repeat for 3-4 layers, and end with shredded cheese on the top. Sprinkle the entire lasagna with Italian seasoning. Bake for 12-15 minutes.

Freedom's Pesto
BASIL, PINE NUTS, AND LEMON JUICE

Place all ingredients in a food processor. Blend until smooth.

4 bunches of basil

1 cup pine nuts

¼ cup lemon juice

¼ cup olive oil

2 cloves garlic

½ teaspoon sea salt

¼ teaspoon black pepper

¼ teaspoon white pepper

Vegetarian

Stuffed Peppers

RED PEPPERS, SPINACH, BLACK BEANS

4 large red peppers

3 cups brown rice, cooked

½ cup chopped spinach

1 small handful shredded carrots

¼ of a red onion, chopped fine

½ of a yellow squash, diced

½ of a zucchini, diced

½ cup broccoli, chopped

⅓ cup black beans, soaked and cooked

Preheat the oven to 350 degrees. Remove the peppers' stems, along with the seeds. Mix up the remaining ingredients. Spoon the ingredients carefully into the peppers. Place the peppers in a baking dish or oven safe covered pan filled with a little water. Cook the peppers covered for 35-40 minutes.

These stuffed peppers always turn out beautifully! To stuff the peppers, use your own creativity and taste buds to guide you; use whatever vegetables you like, along with cooked rice and beans, to create a vegetarian feast. Top completed peppers with spicy cheese sauce.

Spicy Cheese Sauce
JALAPEÑO JACK CHEESE AND HEAVY CREAM

Warm the heavy cream over medium-low heat. Add the remaining ingredients, and stir until the cheese is melted. Pour over the stuffed peppers.

1½ cup heavy cream
8 ounces jalapeño jack cheese
A pinch of crushed red pepper
½ a jalapeño, chopped fine
1 teaspoon garlic powder
Salt and pepper, to taste

Bell peppers are red, yellow, orange, or purple - green are simply unripe colored peppers. Colored peppers are much higher in nutrients than green, even though USDA charts make no differentiation. Always use ripe peppers. Green peppers are not only low in minerals, they are difficult to digest.

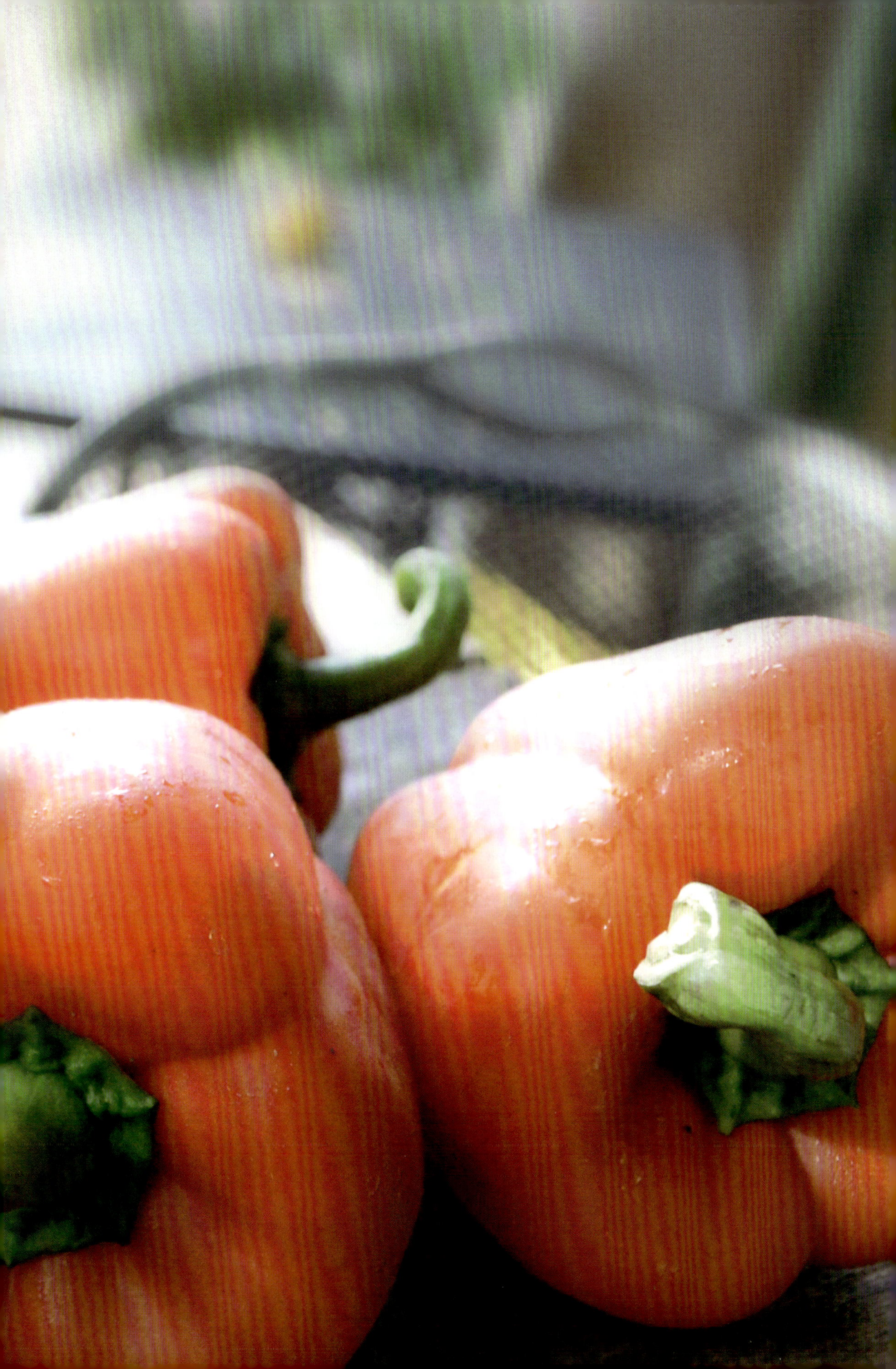

A delightful and filling dish, this lasagna is gluten-free and filled to the brim with colorful vegetables.

Vegetarian Lasagna

BROCCOLI, CARROTS, PEAS

1 box rice lasagna noodles, cooked per directions

The Sauce

2 cups whole milk

½ cup heavy cream

4 tablespoons butter

2 - 3 tablespoons cornstarch dissolved in an equal amount of water

½ teaspoon pepper

½ teaspoon minced garlic

½ teaspoon nutmeg

½ teaspoon white pepper

½ teaspoon salt

Vegetables

½ cup broccoli

½ of a red bell pepper, chopped

1 handful shredded carrots

1 zucchini, diced

½ cup peas

½ cup green beans

2 - 3 tablespoons olive oil

Salt and pepper, to taste

Other Ingredients

2 - 2½ cups mozzarella cheese, shredded

1 bunch spinach, rinsed and chopped

Preheat the oven to 350 degrees. Cook the rice lasagna noodles per the directions on the box. After cooking, place in cool water immediately to prevent the noodles from getting mushy. Then, make the lasagna sauce. Bring milk and cream to a simmer, then whisk in the dry ingredients and cornstarch mixture until the sauce thickens.

In another pot, sauté all the vegetables in the olive oil and salt for 5-6 minutes. Remove the vegetables from the heat, and then put them through in a pasta strainer to remove excess water. Layer cream sauce, pasta, fresh spinach, vegetables, cream sauce (again), and shredded cheese, in that order in a 9 x 13 inch pan. Continue for 3 more layers. Bake the lasagna for 15-20 minutes until cheese is bubbly and golden.

Serve this garbanzo bean burger with all the fixings, including the Cajun sauce (page 108). Delightful and easy to prepare!

Humm-burger
GARBANZO BEANS, POTATOES, AND PARSLEY

2 cups cooked garbanzo beans
2 boiled carrots
4 boiled potatoes
½ of a red onion, diced
½ of a red bell pepper, diced
½ cup parsley, chopped fine
¼ cup green onions, chopped
1 cup whole wheat breadcrumbs
1 teaspoon nutritional yeast
1 - 2 cloves minced garlic
Olive oil for pan frying
Salt and pepper, to taste
Minced garlic, to taste

Soak garbanzo beans overnight, then rinse. Cover with water and bring to a boil. Cook for 45 minutes. Mash the beans, or pulse in a food processor, so that they are still somewhat chunky. Boil the carrots and potatoes together for 20-25 minutes. Mash the carrots and potatoes. Mix all the ingredients together, including the beans and vegetables. Form the mixture into palm-sized burgers. Pan fry the patties in olive oil over medium heat for 4-5 minutes per side. Serve with Cajun sauce, spelt buns, sliced tomato, red onion, and leaves of lettuce.

Cajun Sauce
LEMON JUICE, THYME, CHILI POWDER

Combine all ingredients in a food processor and pulse until smooth.

1 cup mayonnaise
½ cup lemon juice
¼ red onion, chopped
½ teaspoon thyme
½ teaspoon Cajun seasoning
½ teaspoon crushed red pepper
½ teaspoon chili powder
Salt, pepper, and minced garlic, to taste

" Everything in excess is opposed to nature "

- *Hippocrates*

This flavorful, fresh recipe is filling and delicious! It can be made very quickly and easily, without the use of a hot oven. Make this in a pinch as a complete meal. Serve a green salad on the side, if you wish.

Tabouli
BULGER WHEAT, MINT, AVOCADO

Combine the bulgur wheat, warm water, lemon juice, olive oil, and garlic. Let this mixture soak for 20-25 minutes. Add the remaining ingredients and serve!

2 cups bulgur wheat
2 cups warm or hot water
½ cup lemon juice
⅓ cup olive oil
1 teaspoon garlic
1 cucumber, finely diced
½ of a red onion, finely diced
1 whole bunch parsley, finely chopped
1 whole tomato, finely diced
Fresh mint, chopped
Fresh avocado, chopped
Salt and pepper, to taste

Cooking eggplant properly is easy with this delicious dish. Make the eggplant ahead of time, if you like, then create the stacks directly before baking.

Eggplant Parmesan
OLIVE OIL, TOMATO SAUCE, BASIL

2 large eggplants
¼ cup olive oil
½ cup tomato sauce
¼ cup ricotta cheese
⅛ cup Freedom's Pesto Sauce (page 100)
¼ cup mozzarella cheese
1 teaspoon minced garlic
½ teaspoon salt
½ teaspoon black pepper
Parmesan and basil

Preheat oven to 350 degrees. Cut eggplants into slices about ½ an inch thick. Lay them on an oiled cookie sheet. Brush the tops with olive oil, and sprinkle with salt, pepper, garlic, and paprika. Bake for 15-20 minutes. Let the slices cool. Place six of the eggplant slices on a cookie sheet brushed with olive oil. Layer each slice with 1 tablespoon tomato sauce, 1 teaspoon ricotta cheese, ½ teaspoon of Freedom's Pesto Sauce, and a sprinkle of mozzarella. Place another slice of eggplant on the stack, and repeat the layers of ingredients in order. Place a third eggplant slice then sprinkle each with parmesan and basil and bake for an additional 11-15 minutes at 350 degrees.

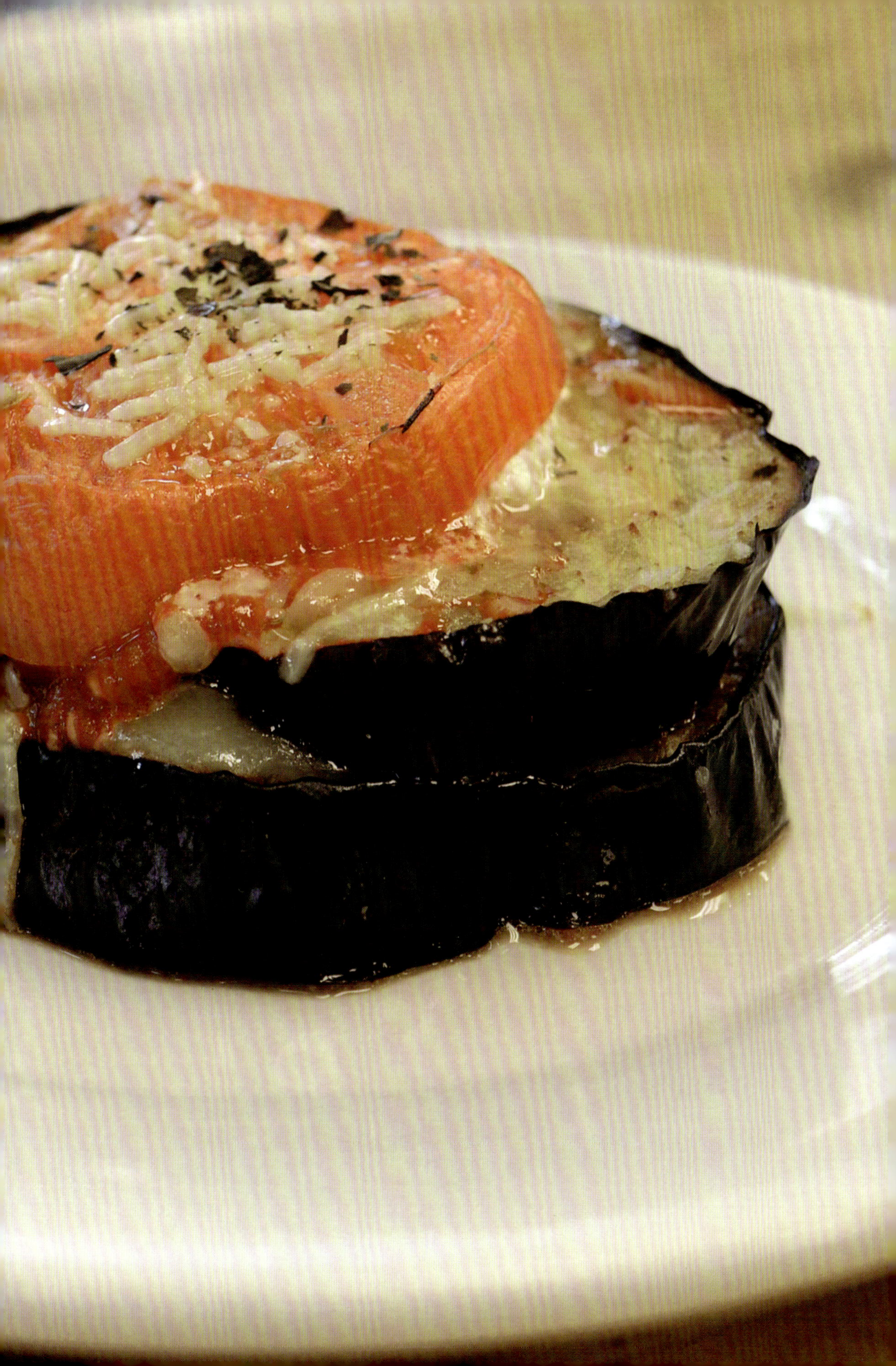

POULTRY

Be sure not to overcook or undercook your chicken dish. Make these recipes your own! Enjoy the flavorful sauces and sautés that accompany each of these simple, delicious recipes.

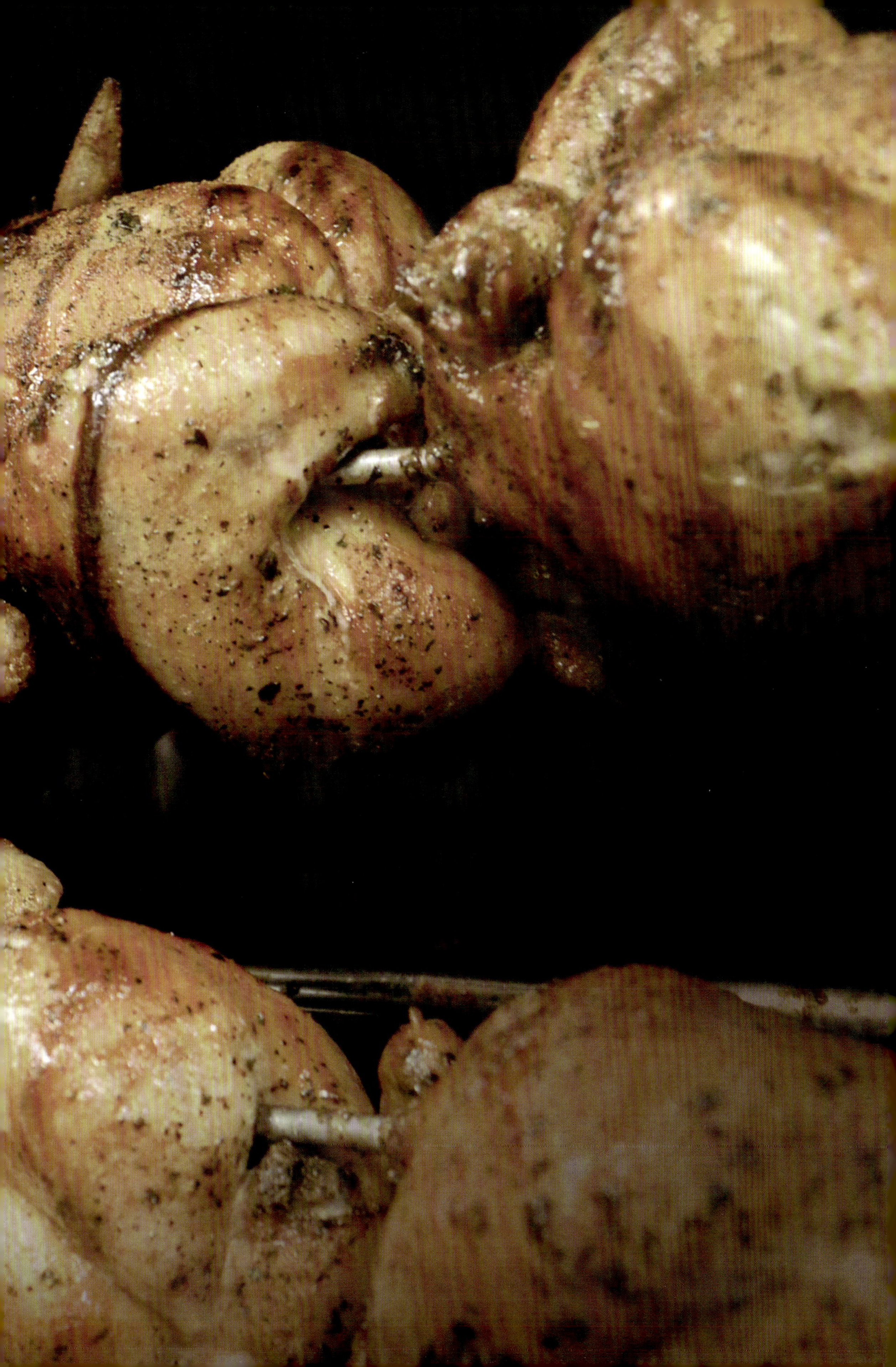

Chicken Enchiladas

SPANISH ONION AND COLBY CHEESE

1 whole chicken
6 - 8 spelt tortilla wraps
1 whole Spanish onion
½ of a red pepper
½ of a green pepper
½ of a yellow pepper
½ cup black beans
½ cup red kidney beans
1 cup shredded cheddar
1 cup shredded colby
Hot sauce, to taste
Enchilada sauce
  (recipe page 117)
Hot salsa, for serving
  (recipe page 118)
Sour cream, for serving

As a vegetarian option, substitute chicken with cooked rice and black beans.

Preheat the oven to 350 degrees. Cook the chicken whole for 35-40 minutes with your choice of seasonings rubbed over top of the chicken. We typically use paprika, garlic, salt and pepper. Shred the entire chicken after it has cooled. Sauté one whole Spanish onion with the peppers for 8-10 minutes. Shred the cheeses. In each of 6-8 spelt tortillas, place a handful of chicken, onions, peppers, cheese, beans, and hot sauce. Fold the sides inwards, then roll. Place in a 9 by 13 inch baking dish. Cover the enchiladas with enchilada sauce, then top with cheese. Bake for 12-15 minutes. Serve with sour cream and salsa on the side.

" Deviation from nature is deviation from happiness "

- *Samuel Johnson*

Enchilada Sauce
RED BELL PEPPER, APPLE CIDER VINEGAR, PAPRIKA

1 red bell pepper
½ cup apple cider vinegar
⅓ cup olive oil
A pinch of salt
A pinch of pepper
1 garlic clove
¼ teaspoon paprika

Roast a red bell pepper in the oven for 10-15 minutes at 350 degrees. Blend it with the remaining ingredients.

We serve enchiladas each week at Food and Thought. You can make them with chicken, or for a vegetarian option, with rice and beans.

Hot Salsa
TOMATOES, JALAPEÑOS, CILANTRO

Brush jalapeños, garlic, and tomatoes with olive oil and salt. Roast them in the oven for 25-30 min at 350 degrees. Blend the roasted vegetables with the cilantro, sea salt, and a bit of water to get the blender going. Simmer the mixture on the stove for about 3-5 minutes. This salsa will keep for 2 weeks in the fridge.

4 tomatoes
3 jalapeños
3 cloves garlic
½ a bunch of cilantro
1 teaspoon sea salt
Olive oil

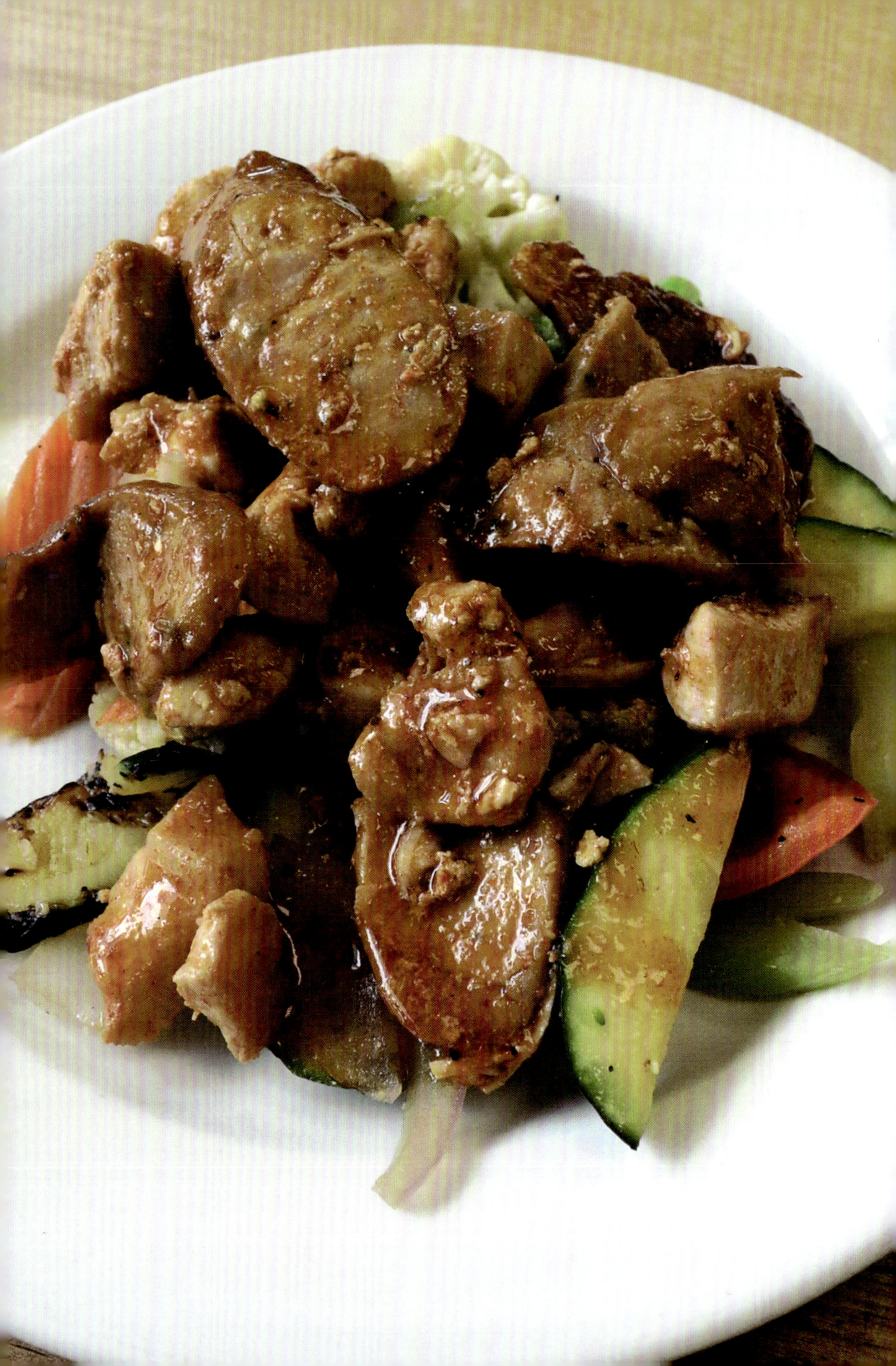

Perhaps one of our most popular poultry entrees, this chicken stir-fry is a simple, complete meal. It takes only about 30-45 minutes to prepare, and it is a delightful, filling feast.

Chicken Stir-Fry

CHICKEN, CELERY, GARLIC

Sauté the chicken breasts in half of the olive oil with the salt, pepper, two of the garlic cloves, and paprika. When the chicken is almost done, add in the chicken turkey sausage. Add the sweet and sour sauce to the chicken mixture. Sauté all of the vegetables in the remaining garlic and olive oil over medium heat for about 10 minutes. Add sea salt and pepper to taste. Place chicken mixture on top of vegetable mixture. Serve with a side of brown rice.

3 chicken breasts, chopped

1 12 ounce package chicken turkey sausage, chopped

3 - 4 tablespoons sweet and sour sauce

½ of a red onion, julienned

2 stalks celery, julienned

1 carrot, julienned

1 stalk broccoli (florets only)

Tri-colored bell peppers, thinly sliced

4 tablespoons olive oil

1 teaspoon paprika

3 - 4 cloves garlic, minced

Salt and pepper, to taste

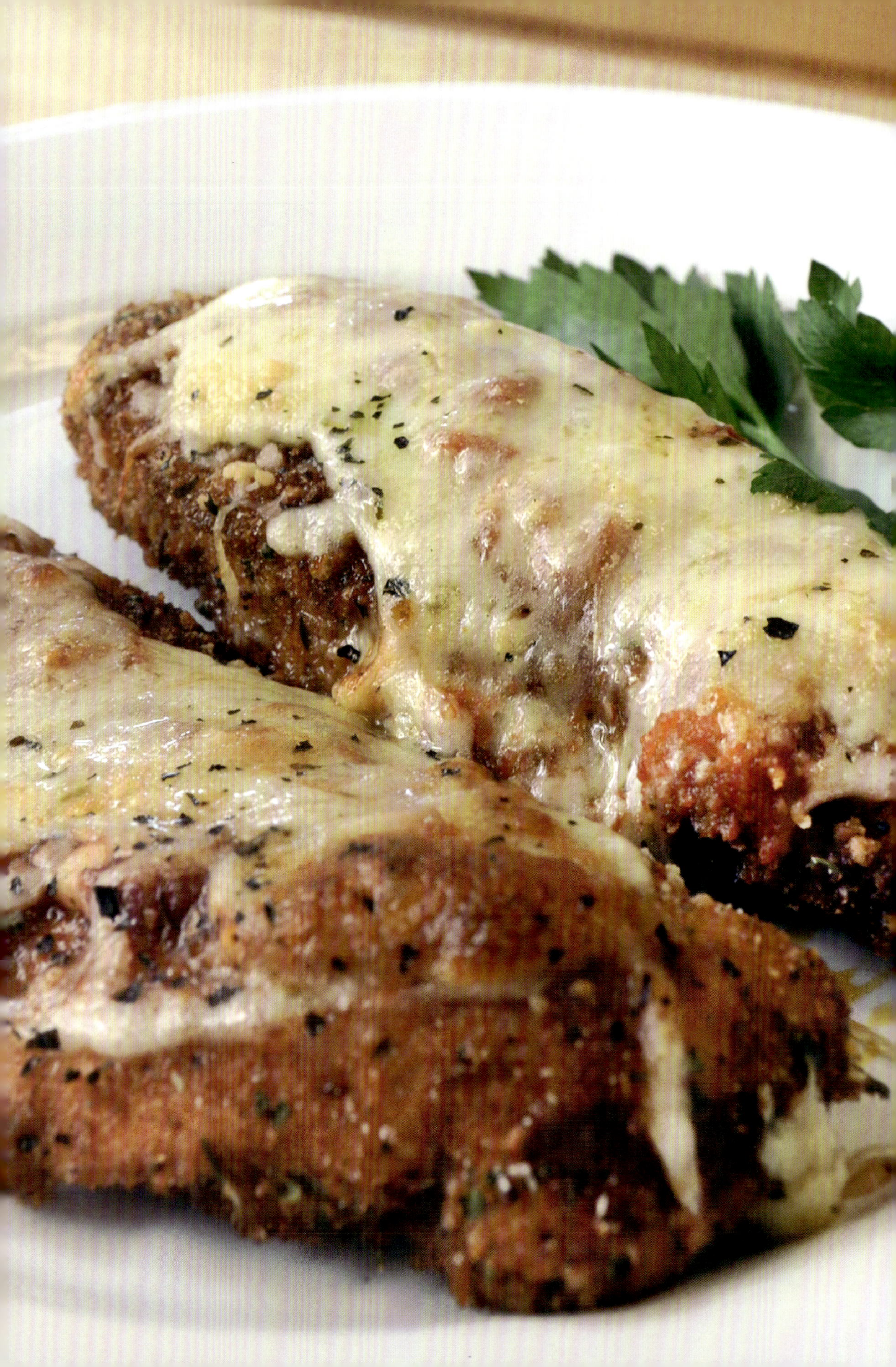

This uncomplicated recipe presents simple, satisfying flavors. Serve with brown rice noodles and steamed greens (page 76).

Chicken Parmesan
MOZZARELLA, PARMESAN, PARSLEY

Preheat the oven to 350 degrees. Filet the chicken breasts down the middle. Beat the egg. Combine bread crumbs, parsley, salt, pepper, and garlic together. Dip each filet in the egg, then coat in the bread crumb mixture. Place in a baking dish brushed with olive oil. Bake the filets in the oven for 20 minutes. Drizzle tomato sauce over each filet, along with shredded mozzarella and parmesan cheese. Top with dried basil. Place the chicken back in the oven for 10-12 minutes, or until the cheese is melted.

3 chicken breasts
1 egg
1 cup mozzarella cheese
½ cup bread crumbs
¼ cup parmesan cheese
¼ cup tomato sauce
1 teaspoon parsley
½ teaspoon minced garlic
Salt and pepper, to taste
Dried basil, to taste

Spanish-Style Chicken

CHICKEN, BELL PEPPERS, CILANTRO

A whole chicken, cut into 8 pieces
3 bell peppers (tricolored), julienned
2 tomatoes, julienned
1 onion, sliced thinly
½ bunch cilantro, chopped
2 tablespoons olive oil
2 teaspoons paprika, divided in two
1 teaspoon cumin, divided in two
4 - 5 cloves minced garlic, divided in two
Salt and pepper, to taste

Preheat the oven to 350 degrees. Cut a whole chicken into eight pieces. Season the chicken with 1 teaspoon paprika, ½ teaspoon of cumin, salt, pepper, and 2 cloves minced garlic. Mix the seasonings together, and rub them over the chicken pieces. Bake the pieces for 35-40 minutes, in a dish covered with a lid or aluminum foil. Sauté the cut vegetables in the olive oil, along with 1 teaspoon paprika, ½ teaspoon of cumin, salt, pepper and 2 cloves minced garlic. Sauté the vegetables over medium heat for about 10 minutes. Add in the chopped cilantro at the very end. Serve the chicken pieces with the vegetables on top.

Serve this dish with brown rice for a complete meal. Flavorful and topped with vegetables - what could be better?

Poultry

" Natural forces within us are the true healers of disease "

- Hippocrates

This chicken dish has a complex flavor and a delicious, creamy sauce. Serve it over coconut basmati rice.

Curry Chicken
COCONUT OIL, CUMIN, SNAP PEAS

Rub the chicken with the curry powder, turmeric, and cumin. Sauté the chicken for 11-15 minutes in the coconut oil. To make the sauce, simmer all of the ingredients over medium low heat for 10-15 minutes. Serve the chicken together with the sauce over coconut basmati rice.

3 chicken breasts
2 tablespoons coconut oil
1 teaspoon curry powder
½ teaspoon (scant) turmeric
½ teaspoon cumin

Sauce

1 can coconut milk
1 teaspoon curry powder
2 carrots, thinly sliced
2 stalks celery, chopped
½ of a red onion, thinly sliced
Tricolored peppers, thinly sliced
½ cup snap peas
¼ bunch of cilantro, chopped
Salt and pepper, to taste

This marinated chicken is delightfully tender and encrusted in a mixture of herbs and spices.

Herb Baked Chicken

ITALIAN SEASONING, THYME, BASIL, OREGANO

1 whole chicken

1 cup flour

½ cup yogurt

1 tablespoon olive oil

½ teaspoon Italian seasoning

½ teaspoon thyme

½ teaspoon basil

½ teaspoon oregano

½ teaspoon parsley flakes

½ teaspoon white pepper

Salt and pepper, to taste

Cut the whole chicken into eight pieces. Rub the yogurt, along with some salt and pepper, all over the pieces. Mix the seasonings all together. Dust the chicken with the flour and seasoning mixture. Allow the chicken to marinate for 1 hour, up to overnight. Preheat the oven to 350 degrees. Brush an 8 by 11 inch baking dish with olive oil. Bake the chicken in the oven for 30 minutes, covered. Uncover the chicken and continue cooking for an additional 15 minutes, until the chicken is golden and crispy.

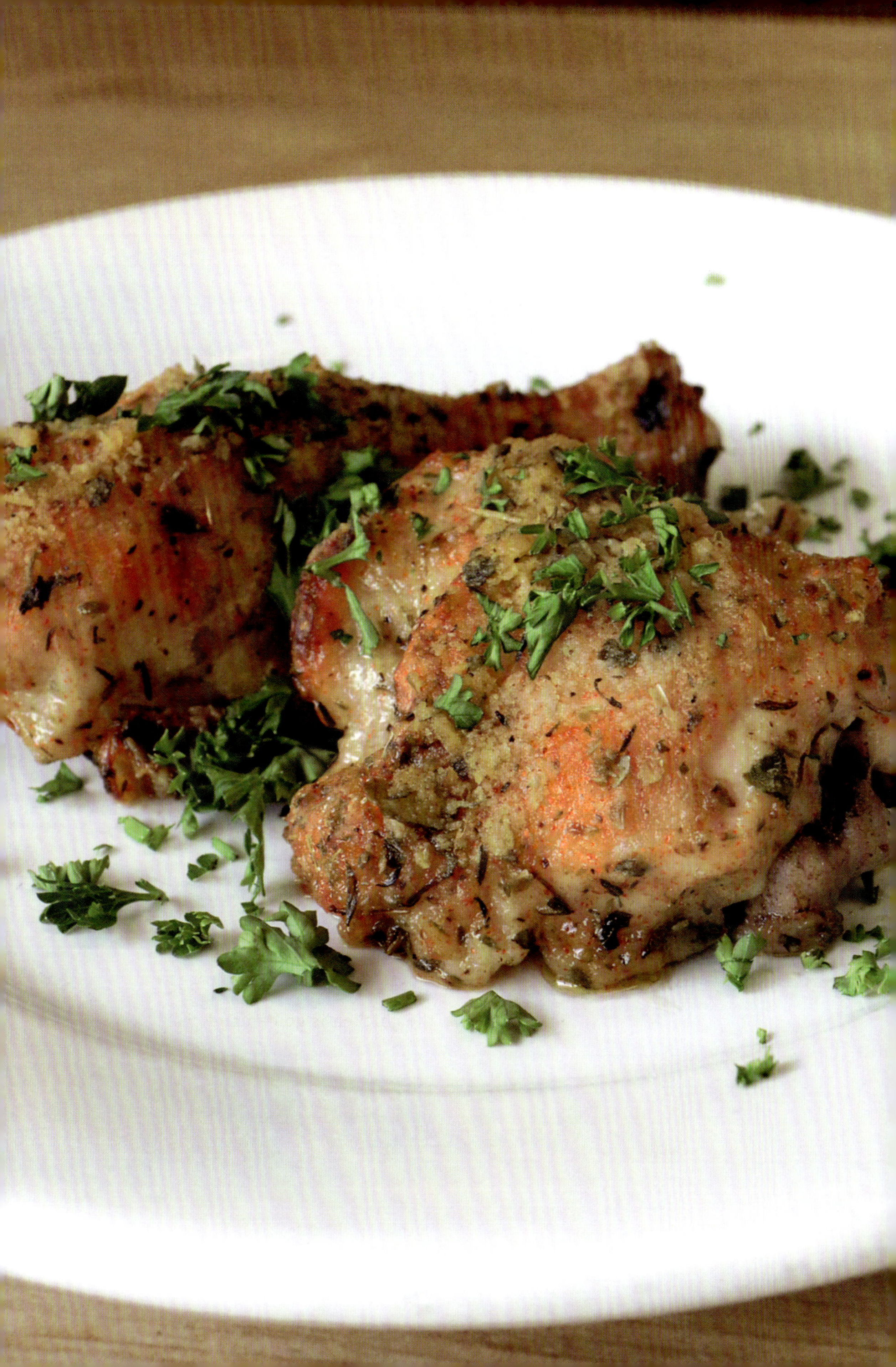

This favorite is reminiscent of a traditional Thanksgiving dinner. We serve our Salisbury steaks with gravy and mashed potatoes each Thursday for lunch and dinner during the summer months. Make this easy, crowd-pleasing dinner for your family.

Turkey Salisbury Steak
BROWN RICE AND MARJORAM

1 pound ground turkey
½ cup brown rice, cooked
⅓ cup red onion, chopped
⅓ cup tricolored bell peppers, chopped (red, yellow, and/or orange)
⅓ bunch of parsley, finely chopped
1 egg
1 - 2 cloves garlic, minced
½ teaspoon marjoram
Salt and pepper, to taste

Preheat oven to 350 degrees. Mix all ingredients together in a bowl, and form into flat patties. Bake the patties for 15 minutes on a pan brushed with olive oil.

Variation - The completed turkey mixture can be made into 10-12 meatballs, or into a meatloaf.

Gravy

VEGETABLE STOCK, GARLIC, SOY SAUCE

Bring the vegetable stock to a boil over medium high, reduce heat to medium low, then whisk in the cornstarch mixture. Stir in the remaining ingredients with a whisk. Add a dash of olive oil and gluten free soy sauce. Simmer together until the mixture thickens a bit.

2 cups of vegetable stock

4 tablespoons cornstarch, mixed into 2 tablespoons of water

2 cloves minced garlic

Salt and pepper, to taste

1 T olive oil

1 T gluten-free soy sauce

SEAFOOD

There is such a product as "Certified Organic Salmon." We do not support this product because it still requires some fairly unnatural techniques to grow the fish, as well as having detrimental environmental impacts. We never serve farm raised fish for myraid reasons - shrimp can be an exception.

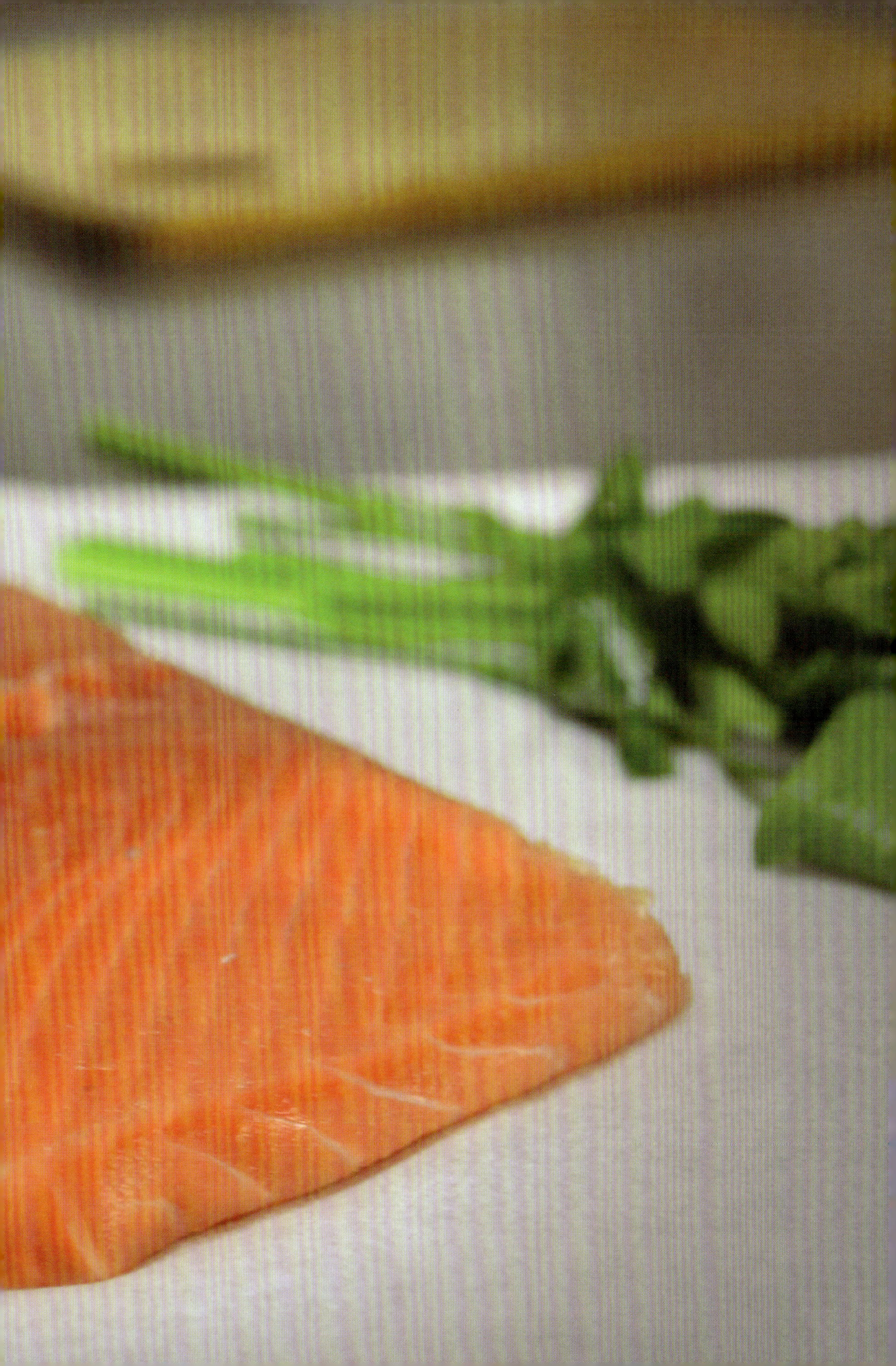

A shrimp stir-fry is a great way to prepare smaller amounts of shrimp. Serve this dish over brown rice or gluten-free rice noodles.

Italian Shrimp Stir-Fry

SHRIMP, WHITE WINE, CHOPPED PARSLEY

- 1 pound of shrimp (about 24-36 pieces), peeled and deveined
- ½ cup white table or cooking wine
- 1 whole tomato, diced
- ½ of a red onion, thinly sliced
- ¼ cup of chopped parsley
- 1 teaspoon minced garlic
- Salt and pepper, to taste

Sauté the garlic, tomato, red onion, and parsley in some olive oil for 3-4 minutes. Add in the shrimp, and cook for 3-5 minutes. Add in the wine. Add sea salt and black pepper to taste. Simmer for an additional minute. Serve over tomato brown rice (page 90).

Similar in nature to fish, the bigger shrimp get, the more bacteria they retain. Choose small shrimp. Shrimp are bottom feeders, so cold water shrimp are best for decreased bacteria content.

Our most popular entrée! Salmon cakes are certainly very tasty. Serve with homemade dill sauce and veggie brown rice (page 88) for a special dinner.

Salmon Cakes
BAKED SALMON, CARROTS, PARSLEY

1 pound salmon

3 carrots

3 potatoes

½ cup bread crumbs

1 egg

½ bunch parsley, chopped

2 stalks celery, diced fine

½ of a red onion, diced fine

½ of a red bell pepper, diced

Flour, to dust cakes

Olive oil, for frying

Sea salt, pepper, and minced garlic, to taste

Variation - Use whatever fish or seafood you like to make these patties. Sub 2 cans of tuna for tuna cakes

Preheat the oven to 350 degrees. Brush a baking dish with olive oil, and sprinkle salt, pepper, and garlic on the piece of salmon. Bake for 8-10 minutes. Boil the carrots and potatoes for about 15 min., or until soft. Mash them with a masher. Add all ingredients to a big bowl, except for the flour and olive oil. Mix together. Form the mixture into salmon cake patties. Dust the cakes in flour. Fry them in a half inch of olive oil on low heat. Cook the patties for about five minutes per side. Finish the patties by placing in the oven on 350 degrees for a few minutes, until golden brown and crisp. Serve immediately with dill sauce. Yields about 8 cakes.

Dill Sauce
SOUR CREAM, LEMON JUICE, DILL

Mix all ingredients together. Stir the mixture, and taste it. Add more dill or seasonings as needed. Serve with the salmon cakes.

1½ cups sour cream

½ cup lemon juice

1 teaspoon dill

A pinch of garlic powder

A pinch of black pepper

A pinch of salt

Mahi Mahi Bites

MAHI MAHI, MINCED GARLIC, PAPRIKA

1½ pounds mahi mahi, cut in chunks
½ cup whole wheat bread crumbs
1 teaspoon garlic powder
1 teaspoon paprika
½ teaspoon sea salt
½ teaspoon pepper
olive oil

Preheat the oven to 350 degrees. Season the mahi mahi chunks with garlic, paprika, salt and pepper. Dust the pieces of fish with the bread crumbs. Bake for 10-12 minutes in a pan brushed with olive oil.

These delightful morsels are baked in the oven with a layer of breadcrumbs, sealing in the moisture and creating a tender, flavorful finished product.

Tartar Sauce
MAYONNAISE, WORCESTERSHIRE SAUCE, RED ONION

While the fish is in the oven, combine all the tartar sauce ingredients. Serve with the mahi mahi bites.

1 cup mayonnaise

¼ of a red onion, diced

1 tablespoon cucumber relish

1 tablespoon apple cider vinegar

1 teaspoon Worcestershire sauce

½ teaspoon paprika

½ teaspoon minced garlic

Salt and pepper, to taste

Yummy and gluten-free, the cornbread cod pairs excellently with the avocado salsa (page 140). Enjoy it with a mixed baby greens salad.

Cornbread Cod

COD, CORNMEAL, LEMON PEPPER

1½ pounds cod
1 cup cornmeal
1 teaspoon thyme
1 teaspoon lemon pepper
½ teaspoon paprika
½ teaspoon minced garlic
Salt and pepper, to taste

Preheat your oven to 350 degrees. Combine the cornmeal with all other spices. Dust the cod in the cornmeal mixture. Lay the fish on a pan brushed with olive oil. Drizzle some additional oil over top of the fish. Bake for 12-15 minutes.

Making your own bread crumbs is so easy! Simply take pieces of bread (we use the ends of the loaves of sandwich bread), and put them on a pan. Place the pan in the oven and bake for 10-15 minutes. Then place the pieces of bread in a food processor and pulse.
Voila – bread crumbs!

Avocado Salsa
AVOCADO, CILANTRO, LEMON JUICE

Spoon the avocado into the bowl, and add in all other ingredients. Mix together, and then serve with the cornbread cod.

Prepare this salsa with hass avocados or Florida avocados. Use it as a topping for the cornbread cod or with corn chips as an appetizer.

3 avocados, diced
1 tomato, chopped
½ of a sweet onion, chopped
¼ bunch of cilantro, chopped fine
½ cup lemon juice
Salt, to taste
Cayenne pepper, to taste (optional)

Sweet and tangy, this salmon recipe is a flavorful twist on traditional baked salmon.

Honey Orange Glazed Salmon

ORANGE JUICE, HONEY, CANDIED GINGER

1½ pounds salmon

1 cup orange juice

⅓ cup honey

2 - 3 tablespoons orange spread or marmalade

A sprinkle of cilantro flakes

A sprinkle of candied ginger

Salt and pepper, to taste

Preheat your oven to 350 degrees. Whisk together the orange juice, honey, orange marmalade, and salt and pepper. Brush a baking dish with olive oil. Drizzle the mixture over the salmon. Sprinkle candied ginger and cilantro over the salmon as well. Bake for 10-12 minutes. Place an orange slice and parsley on top of the salmon to garnish.

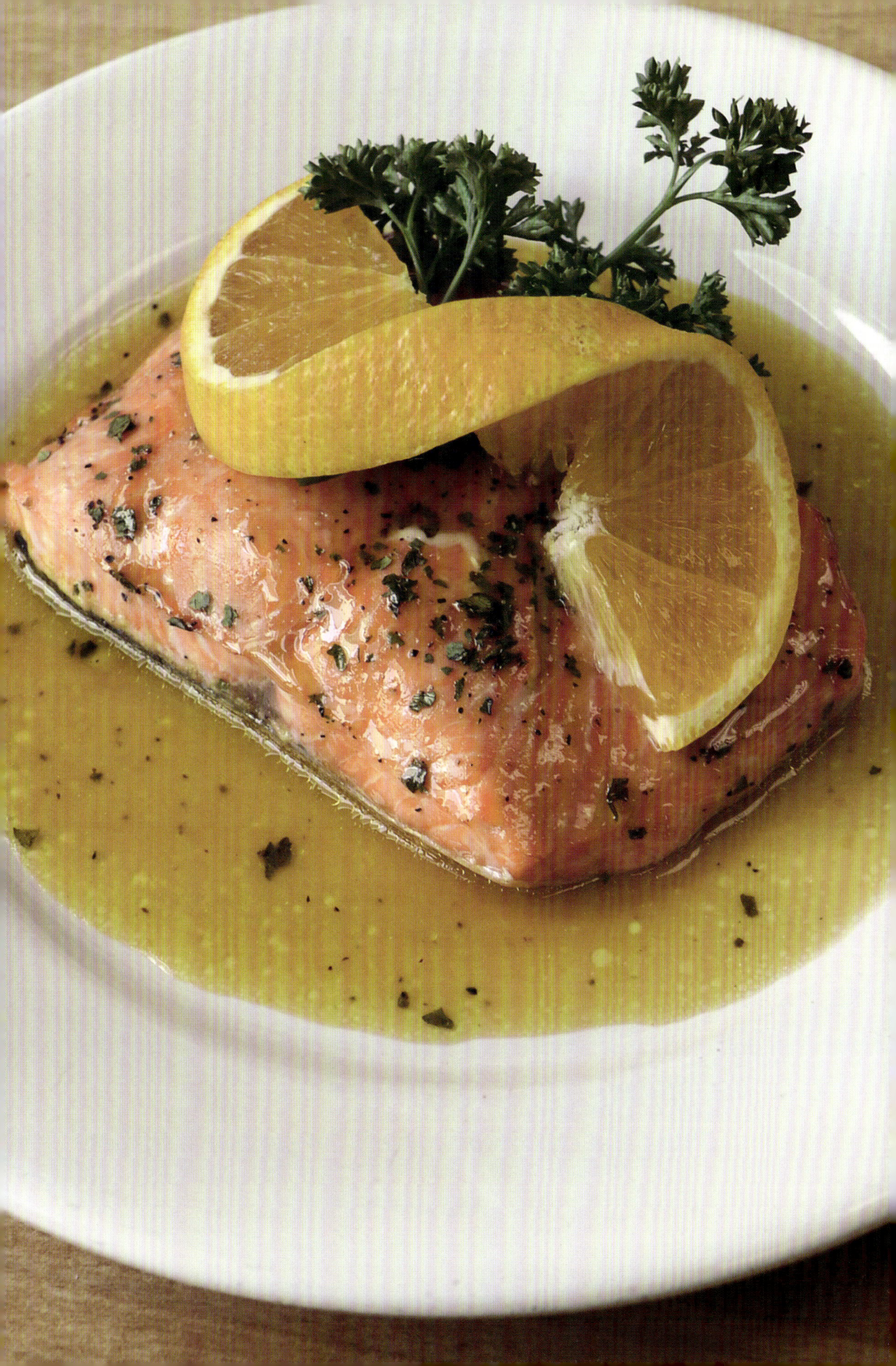

Baked Cod
COLDWATER COD, OLIVE OIL, GARLIC

1½ pound coldwater cod

Olive oil

Minced garlic

Salt and pepper

Preheat the oven to 350 degrees. Place the cod in an oven safe baking dish brushed with olive oil. Sprinkle each four ounce piece of cod with salt, pepper and minced garlic. Drizzle olive oil over the fish. Bake in the oven for 10-12 minutes.

Rich with color, this flavorful slaw pairs well with the baked cod or any other white fish, providing a light and colorful meal, rich in protein and vitamins.

Asian Slaw
AVOCADO, CILANTRO, LEMON JUICE

Shred the cabbage. Slice the carrots, onion and red pepper in thin strips (julienne). Chop the green onions. Place all the vegetables in a large bowl and add in remaining ingredients. Serve a healthy portion on the side of the baked cod.

½ of a cabbage
2 - 3 carrots
½ of a red pepper
¼ of a red onion
¼ cup purple cabbage
2 green onions
¼ cup agave nectar
¼ cup rice vinegar
2 tablespoons toasted sesame oil
½ teaspoon crushed red pepper
A sprinkle of black sesame seeds
Salt and pepper, to taste

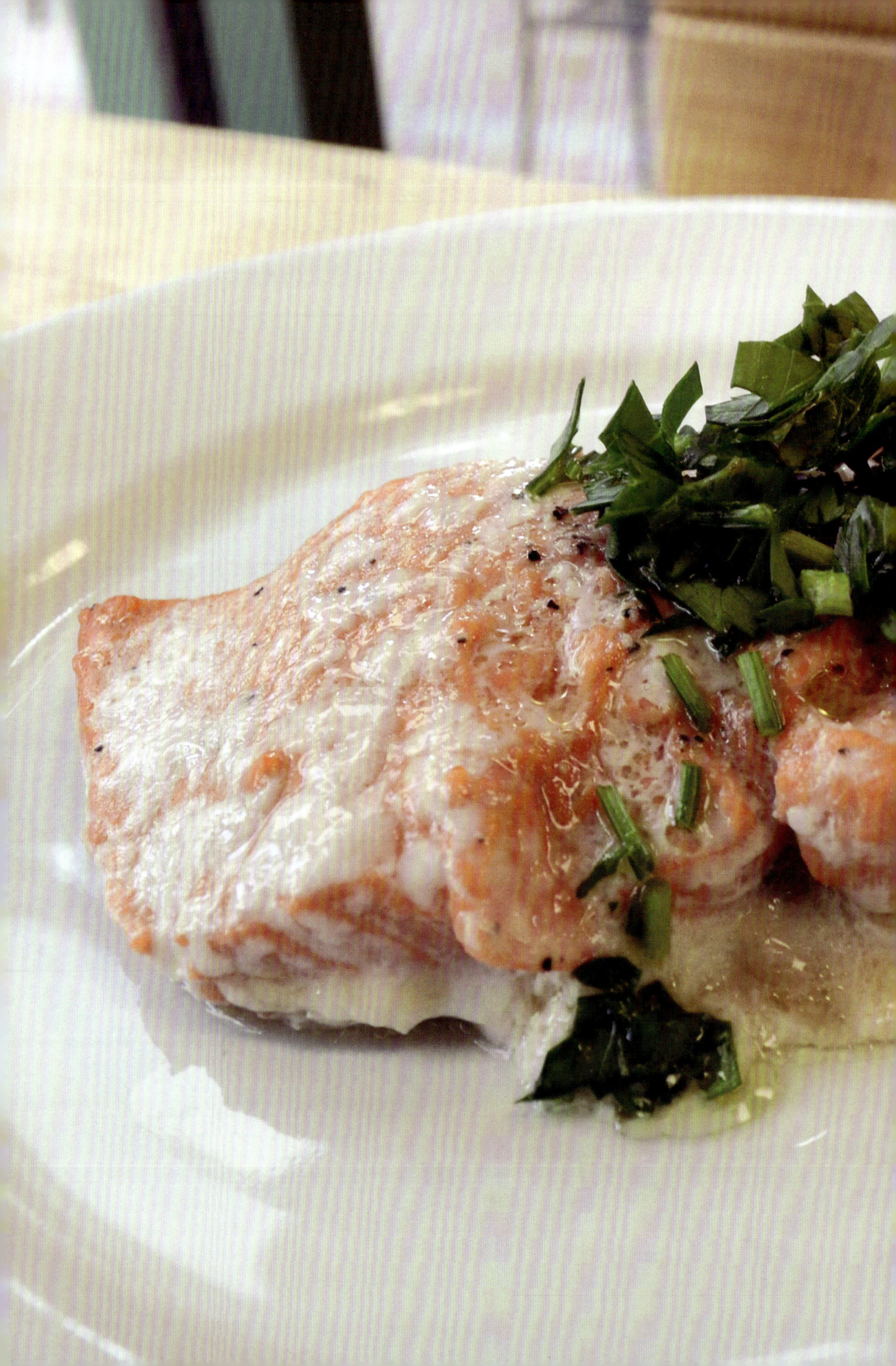

This simple salmon dish brings out the flavor of the fish. For sides, try the steamed greens (page 76) and hazelnut feta quinoa salad (page 52).

Garlic Butter Salmon
SALMON, WHITE WINE, MINCED GARLIC

Preheat the oven to 350 degrees. Cover the salmon with the wine. Put minced garlic, salt and pepper over top of the salmon. Place a pad of butter on top of each portion of salmon, or drizzle olive oil on top of each piece. Bake the salmon covered for 10-12 minutes. Garnish with chopped parsley or chives.

1½ pounds salmon (4 pieces)
½ cup white wine
Minced garlic, to taste
2 T butter or olive oil
Salt and pepper, to taste

This favorite is perfect for mid-summer when raspberries are in season. Make the preserves from scratch, or use organic raspberry preserves for the sauce.

Raspberry Glazed Mahi Mahi

MAHI MAHI, RED ONION, RASPBERRIES

1½ pounds mahi mahi

½ stick of butter

½ of a red onion

8 ounces of raspberries (save a few out for garnish)

½ cup of raspberry preserves

Preheat the oven to 350 degrees. Sauté the red onion in the butter with a pinch of salt and pepper. Add in the raspberries, along with the raspberry preserves. Simmer for 3-5 minutes. Place on top of the fish, and then bake in the oven uncovered for 10-15 minutes. Garnish the finished fish with a few whole raspberries.

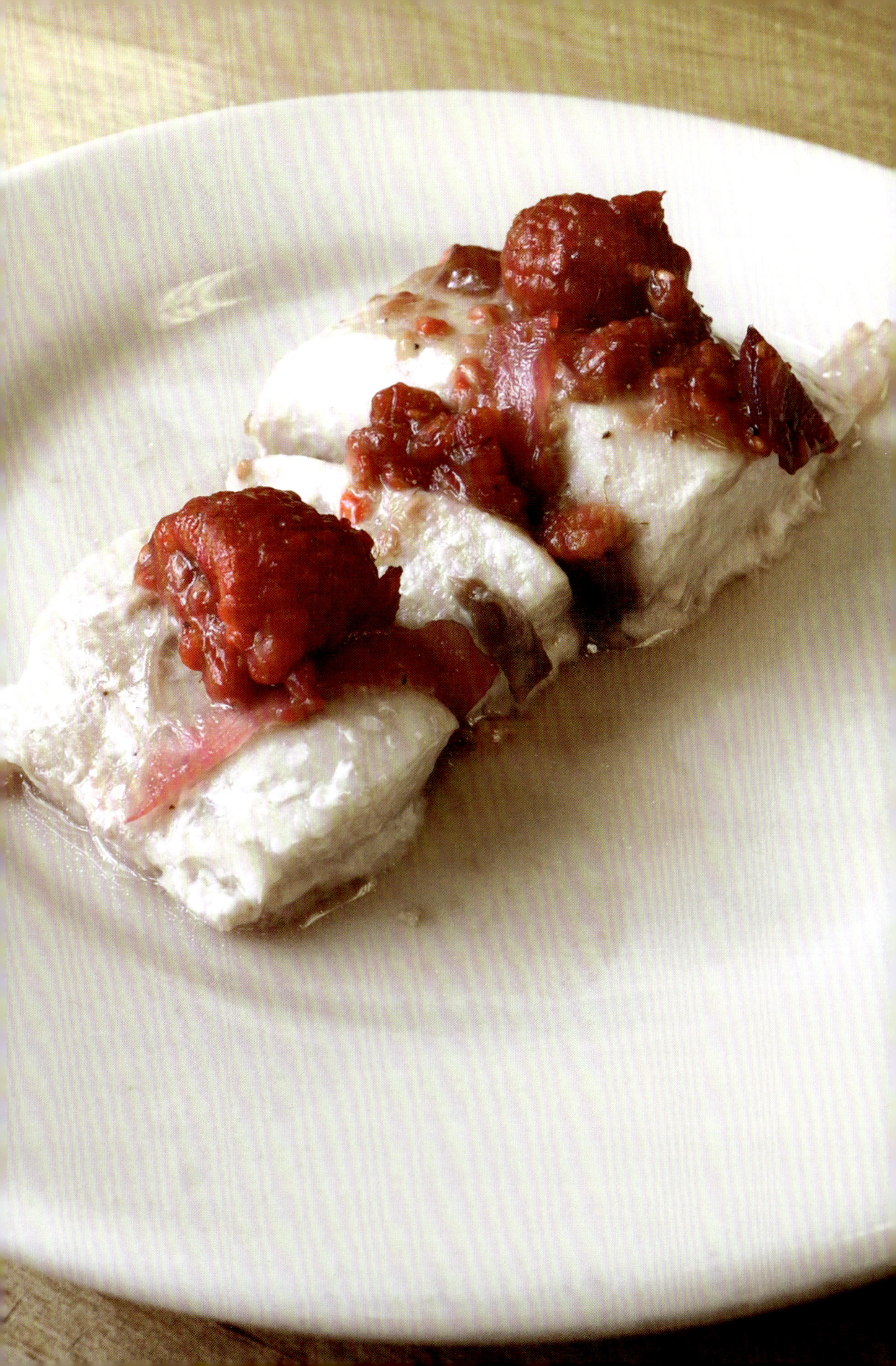

Enjoy this fish recipe topped with the pineapple mango salsa, or place both the fish and salsa in taco shells and top with lettuce and tomato for a delicious meal.

Baked Coconut Mahi Mahi

SHREDDED COCONUT, BROWN SUGAR, COCONUT OIL

1½ pounds Mahi Mahi

¼ cup shredded coconut

1 teaspoon Chinese 5 Spice

A pinch of brown sugar

Coconut oil

Sea salt

Preheat the oven to 350 degrees. Brush the coconut oil on the bottom of a baking dish. Sprinkle the shredded coconut, spices and sugar on top of the fish. Bake for 12-15 minutes.

Pineapple Mango Salsa

MANGO, PINEAPPLE, LEMON JUICE

Combine all the ingredients.
Serve the salsa on top of the fish.

1 mango, chopped
½ of a pineapple, cored and diced
¼ of a red onion, diced
½ cup cilantro, chopped
⅓ cup red bell pepper, chopped
½ cup lemon juice
Salt and pepper, to taste

Seafood

OUR MISSION

"You must be the change you wish to see in the world" - Ghandi

To first practice what we preach, by being responsible for our own well-being, which in turn increases the well-being of our neighbors and our planet. To shed light on the profound advantages of simplicity, self-sufficiency, and self-reliance. To help make evident that solutions to all problems, great and small, are found in us as individuals, not in countries, political parties, or social movements.

"Deviation from nature is deviation from happiness" - Samuel Johnson

To help create a better understanding of the need to live in accordance with the dictates of nature. To demonstrate by our own practices and products how absurd the notion that chemicals and toxins are necessary to grow our food, or that drugs are necessary to maintain health. To offer WITHOUT EXCEPTION only food that is grown sustainably and organically.

"The mind is not a vessel to be filled, but a fire to be kindled" - Plutarch

To make available information that is difficult to find or non-existent in today's corporate driven media, and to share it openly and readily to all who wish to take control of their own health and well-being.

OUR GOAL

To make everyone who works here and everyone who shops here a happier, healthier, and more self-reliant person.

INDEX

A

Apples
    The Doctor, 11
Asian Slaw, 144
Avocado
    Asian Slaw, 144
    Avocado Salsa, 140
    Spicy Guacamole, 49
Ayurvedic Proverb, 50

B

Baked Coconut Mahi Mahi, 149
Baked Cod, 143
Banana
    Berry Nice, 13
    The Gentle Joe, 16
    Sprouted Banana Nut Muffins, 30
Beans
    Black Beans, 91
    Homemade Hummus, 44
    Humm-burger, 107
    Lentil Stew, 61
    Minestrone, 62
    soaking, 61
Beets
    Pickled Beet Salad, 41
Berry Nice, 15
Breakfast Quiche, 21
Broccoli
    Chicken Stir-Fry, 120
    Stuffed Peppers, 101
    Vegetarian Lasagna, 103
    Veggie Saute, 77
Brown Basmati Rice
    Coconut Brown Rice, 85
Brown Rice Spaghetti Noodles
    Chicken Noodle Soup, 72
Bulgur Wheat
    Tabouli, 110

Buttermilk
    Gluten-Free Chocolate Chia Muffins, 26
    Sprouted Pancakes, 24

C

Cabbage
    Asian Slaw, 144
    Costa Rican Cole Slaw, 56
    Veggie Brown Rice, 88
    Veggie Saute, 77
Cajun Sauce, 108
Carrots
    Sprouted Carrot Muffins, 32
Cheese
    Breakfast Quiche, 21
    Chicken Enchiladas, 115
    Chicken Parmesan, 122
    choosing, 8
    Eggplant Boats, 98
    Italian Lasagna, 99
    Spicy Cheese Sauce, 102
    Vegetarian Lasagna, 103
Chia Powder
    Gluten-Free Chocolate Chia Muffins, 26
Chicken Dishes
    Chicken Enchiladas, 115
    Chicken Noodle Soup, 72
    Chicken Parmesan, 122
    Chicken Stir-Fry, 120
    Curry Chicken, 126
    Grape Walnut Chicken Salad, 35
    Herb Baked Chicken, 127
    Spanish-Style Chicken, 123
Coconut Brown Rice, 85
Cod
    Baked Cod, 143
    choosing, 8
    Cornbread Cod, 139
Costa Rican Cole Slaw, 56

Cucumber
    The Green Machine, 14
    Tabouli, 110
Curry Chicken, 126

D

The Doctor, 11
Dill Sauce, 136

E

Eggplant
    Eggplant Boats, 98
    Eggplant Parmesan, 111
Eggs
    Breakfast Quiche, 21
    choosing, 22
    Spanish-Style Eggs, 27
Enchilada Sauce, 117

F

Fish Dishes
    Baked Coconut Mahi Mahi, 149
    Baked Cod, 143
    choosing, 8
    Cornbread Cod, 139
    Garlic Butter Salmon, 146
    Honey Orange Glazed Salmon, 141
    Italian Shrimp Stir-Fry, 133
    Mahi Mahi Bites, 137
    Salmon Cakes, 135
    Raspberry Glazed Mahi Mahi, 147
Freedom Fries, 82
Freedom's Pesto, 100

G

Garbanzo Beans
    Garbanzo Bean Stew, 61
    Homemade Hummus, 44
    Humm-burger, 107
Garlic Butter Salmon, 146
The Gentle Joe, 18

Ginger
    The Doctor, 11
    The Green Machine, 14
Gluten-Free
    Breakfast Quiche, 21
    Chicken Noodle Soup, 72
    Cornbread Cod, 139
    Gluten-Free Chocolate Chia
        Muffins, 26
    Italian Lasagna, 99
    Vegetarian Lasagna, 105
Gluten-Free Chocolate
    Chia Muffins, 26
Grape Walnut Chicken Salad, 35
Gravy, 130
The Green Machine, 14

H

Hazelnut Feta Quinoa Salad, 52
Herb Baked Chicken, 127
Hippocrates, 31, 75, 79, 87, 109, 125
Homemade Hummus, 44
Honey Orange Glazed Salmon, 141
Hot Salsa, 118
Humm-burger, 107

I

Italian Lasagna, 99
Italian Shrimp Stir-Fry, 133

J

Jalapeno
    Costa Rican Cole Slaw, 56
    Hot Salsa, 118
    Pico de Gallo, 48
    Mexican Tuna Salad, 40
    Spicy Guacamole, 49
Juices
    The Doctor, 11
    The Green Machine, 14
Juvenal, 14

K
Katie's Sprouted Apple Bread, 32

L
Lentil Stew, 61

M
Mahi Mahi
   Baked Coconut Mahi Mahi, 149
   Mahi Mahi Bites, 137
   Raspberry Glazed Mahi Mahi, 147
Mashed Potatoes, 80
Meats
   choosing, 7
Mexican Tuna Salad, 40
Milk
   choosing, 8
Minestrone, 64

P
Pasta Salad, 38
Peas
   Chicken Noodle Soup, 72
   Curry Chicken, 126
   Turkey Rice Soup, 69
   Vegetable Soup, 60
   Vegetarian Lasagna, 105
   Veggie Brown Rice, 88
Peppers
   choosing, 103
   Eggplant Boats, 98
   Pasta Salad, 38
   Stuffed Peppers, 101
   Zucchini Crusted Pizza, 95-96
Pickled Beet Salad, 41
Pico de Gallo, 48
Pine Nuts, 100
Pineapple Mango Salsa, 150
Potatoes
   Freedom Fries, 82

Potatoes, *continued*
   Humm-burger, 107
   Lentil Stew, 61
   Mashed Potatoes, 80
   Potato Salad, 53
   Potato Leek Soup, 65
   Salmon Cakes, 135
   Turkey Rice Soup, 69
   Vegetable Soup, 60
Pumpkin Soup, 68

R
Raspberry Glazed Mahi Mahi, 147
Rice
   Coconut Brown Rice, 85
   Eggplant Boats, 98
   Stuffed Peppers, 101
   Tomato Brown Rice, 90
   Turkey Rice Soup, 69
   Veggie Brown Rice, 88
Ricotta Cheese
   Eggplant Parmesan, 111
   Italian Lasagna, 99

S
Salads
   Costa Rican Cole Slaw, 56
   Grape Walnut Chicken Salad, 35
   Hazelnut Feta Quinoa Salad, 52
   Homemade Hummus, 44
   Mexican Tuna Salad, 40
   Pasta Salad, 38
   Pickled Beet Salad, 41
   Pico de Gallo, 48
   Potato Salad, 53
   Spanish Fruit Salad, 45
   Spicy Guacamole, 49
Salmon
   choosing, 7
   Garlic Butter Salmon, 146
   Honey Orange Glazed Salmon, 141

Salmon, *continued*
    Salmon Cakes, 135
Salt
    choosing, 7
Salsa
    Avocado Salsa, 140
    Hot Salsa, 118
    Pico de Gallo, 48
    Pineapple Mango Salsa, 150
Samuel Johnson, 116
Sauces
    Cajun Sauce, 108
    Dill Sauce, 136
    Enchilada Sauce, 117
    Freedom's Pesto, 100
    Gravy, 130
    Spicy Cheese Sauce, 102
    Tartar Sauce, 138
Shrimp
    Italian Shrimp Stir-Fry, 133
Smoothies
    Berry Nice, 14
    The Gentle Joe, 18
Soup
    Chicken Noodle Soup, 72
    Lentil Stew, 61
    Minestrone, 64
    Potato Leek Soup, 65
    Pumpkin Soup, 68
    Turkey Rice Soup, 69
    Vegetable Soup, 60
Spanish Fruit Salad, 45
Spanish-Style Chicken, 123
Spanish-Style Eggs, 27
Spicy Cheese Sauce, 102
Spicy Guacamole, 49
Spinach
    The Green Machine, 14
    Steamed Greens, 76
    Stuffed Peppers, 101
    Vegetarian Lasagna, 105
    Zucchini Crusted Pizza, 95-96

Sprouted Banana Nut Muffins, 30
Sprouted Flour, 6
Sprouted Pancakes, 24
Steamed Greens, 76
Stuffed Peppers, 101
Sweet Potatoes
    Sweet Potato Patties, 83
    Vegetable Soup, 60

T
Tabouli, 110
Tartar Sauce, 138
Tomato Brown Rice, 90
Turkey
    Turkey Rice Soup, 69
    Turkey Salisbury Steak, 129

V
Vegetable Soup, 60
Vegetarian Dishes
    Eggplant Parmesan, 111
    Humm-burger, 107
    Italian Lasagna, 99
    Stuffed Peppers, 101
    Vegetarian Lasagna, 105
    Zucchini Crusted Pizza, 95-96
Veggie Brown Rice, 88
Veggie Saute, 77

W
Walnuts
    Grape Walnut Chicken Salad, 35
    Spanish Fruit Salad, 45
    Sprouted Banana Nut Muffins, 30

Z
Zucchini
    Chicken Noodle Soup, 72
    Vegetable Soup, 60
    Vegetarian Lasagna, 105
    Veggie Saute, 77
    Zucchini Crusted Pizza, 95-96

Edited by Anna Snyder. Photography and design by Becca Perhay & Oliver Denson.